"Christian brings a raw, vulnerable gift to the women of her generation, and that's the unyielding truth of the only source of unshakable power and confidence—our heavenly Father and the work done for us by Jesus Christ. This call is a challenge I pray we're all brave enough to accept, rejecting the lies the world tells us, finding our wholeness through the grace of God alone, and embracing the life-giving message that we are enough because we are His. Christian is not only my family, but she is also a friend and author I admire and adore. Her authenticity is refreshing and relatable and will no doubt change the hearts and perspectives of all readers."

Madison Prewett Troutt, bestselling author and TV personality

"Many years ago, a woman who was older and much wiser than me encouraged me to let my past be my teacher and my future be my friend. Decades later her insight still rings true. Far too many people are so trapped in the wounds and disappointments of their past that they can't seem to find their path forward. *Break Up with What Broke You* is woven with stories and practical ways to glean the lessons, redeem the mistakes, and leave behind the shame. I love how my beautiful and brave daughter-in-love, Christian Bevere, has crafted a message that invites young women to journey forward."

Lisa Bevere, *New York Times* bestselling author of
Without Rival

"Christian's words speak to the heart with keen understanding and powerful depth. These pages are full of encouragement for any woman who believes God has called her to more than what she's left in her past."

Rebekah Lyons, author of *Rhythms of Renewal*

"I am pleased Christian is exposing the enemy of shame, the quiet monster holding so many captive. This hidden foe removes our hope—the oxygen of our souls, without which we lose all motivation to live with purpose. Jesus came to deliver us from shame, and

T0035322

when we understand what He did for us, the tethers of condemnation are severed. This book will shed insight into the freedom He provides. I have the privilege of being lovely Christian's father-in-law and have come to know her as a woman of virtue and noble character. She has a story to tell, and I believe in hearing her story, many will be led to freedom."

John Bevere, bestselling author and minister; cofounder of
Messenger International

"Through vulnerable testimony and practical advice, Christian shows us how to break up with what's kept us chained to our past. Her writing is a powerful tool for silencing the lies of shame and living in the freedom God has provided for us."

Alex Seeley, lead pastor of The Belonging Co; author of
Tailor Made

"As a relationship consultant, I've seen the detriment that living under shame can bring. For those of you who believe that your past defines your future, Christian Bevere's message of redemption and hope is the book you've been waiting for! It's a must-read!"

Dr. Morgan Cutlip, author and psychotherapist

BREAK UP WITH WHAT BROKE YOU

BREAK UP WITH WHAT BROKE YOU

How God Redeems and
Rewrites Your Story

CHRISTIAN BEVERE

Revell
a division of Baker Publishing Group
Grand Rapids, Michigan

© 2023 by Christian Bevere

Published by Revell
a division of Baker Publishing Group
Grand Rapids, Michigan
www.revellbooks.com

Printed in the United States of America

Library of Congress Cataloging-in-Publication Data
Names: Bevere, Christian, 1995– author.
Title: Break up with what broke you : how God redeems and rewrites your story /
    Christian Bevere.
Description: Grand Rapids, Michigan : Revell, a division of Baker Publishing
    Group, [2023]
Identifiers: LCCN 2023002066 | ISBN 9780800742133 (paperback) | ISBN
    9780800743086 (casebound) | ISBN 9781493441242 (ebook)
Subjects: LCSH: Christian women—Religious life. | Suffering—Religious
    aspects—Christianity.
Classification: LCC BV4527 .B4835 2023 | DDC 248.8/43—dc23/eng/20230315
LC record available at https://lccn.loc.gov/2023002066

To my little sisters,
may your lives be rich in beauty
and laced in the wholeness
God's woven for you.

Contents

THE
BREAK
DOWN

Part 1

Ready the release.

Uproot the weeds impeding your growth,
the barriers keeping you from your betrothed.

Roll the dice, take a gamble in faith—
you won't be abandoned, you won't be scathed.

Be intimate with brokenness,
for wholeness will accompany the act.
Any damage assessed and addressed
will heal if allowed to extract.

These pinpricks trickle a purposeful relief,
releasing the grips of the enemy—the liar, the thief.

Through fists clenched and knuckles pale,
let go, breathe, and know his plans are derailed.

You are healing.
You are releasing.
You are uncovering.
You are liberating.

Be brave now; break down every piece that's
stolen your hope, your security, and your peace.

01. What Broke You?

The wound is the place where the Light enters you.

—Rumi

A major breakthrough. That first big break. These triumphs aren't reserved for only professionals and the elite. Even the hard-pressed obtain vitality through living out their purpose. Stories of significance and grandeur are still being written—or rewritten—today.

If you've been broken, you can have a breakthrough.

The Author of the universe has more ahead for you. Moving through the very things that held you back will lead to the ability to move on from the past.

We're broken people. But broken things rebuild stronger. We do not need to fear, for Christ made a way for us to be restored completely in Him as His own body was broken on the cross.

All the broken and dislocated pieces of the universe—people and things, animals and atoms—get properly fixed and fit together in vibrant harmonies, all because of his death, his blood that poured down from the cross. (Col. 1:20 MSG)

Naturally broken things are tossed aside without a second thought. But our Creator doesn't love us naturally. His supernatural grace redeems and rewrites our story, fashioning and mending us anew.

We're going to break down what's left you feeling broken.
We're going to break away from the pain of the past.
We're going to break through to the promises of the future.
But all this depends on you. Because breakthrough is a noun and a verb, a promise and an action. You need to allow yourself transformation.

You need to break up with what broke you.

Faulty Foundations

Not all homes are built the same, but each follows a blueprint that requires a strong base. Pretty exteriors can't rectify broken interiors. You could have a structure as grand as the Taj Mahal or as eye-catching as the Palace of Versailles, yet the entire construction would be at risk of destruction if the foundation were out of line. This rings true with our inner health as well—some of us are good at masking what's going on under the surface and putting on a pretty smile. On the outside we look fine, but deep down something is off. Just like in a home with a faulty foundation, the longer we put off getting down to the core of what's shifted and misaligned, the more it'll cost. It takes only one little loose brick to cause a slope.

Interestingly, the homes you'd think would have issues aren't always the ones that do. Many buyers shy away from purchasing an older house and opt for one built in the last ten years in the hopes of getting a better-built, longer-standing home. But sometimes the homes with the most issues are the newer models. Many older homes boast master craftsmanship and quality materials that will outlast and outshine some of their younger neighbors. You may think, *But I'm not broken.* Or *I shouldn't feel broken. I have great friends, a good life, and everything looks good on the surface, so I'm good.*

The book of Hebrews tells us, "For every house is built by someone, but God is the builder of everything. . . . And we are his house, if indeed we hold firmly to our confidence and the hope in which we glory" (3:4, 6). Tending to the structure and rebuilding when and where needed ensures a home's longevity. We can do the same for our inner structure. Take the journey of this book to dive deep into your emotions, history, character, and hopes, and ask yourself, "What's been broken and could use some rebuilding?" It doesn't mean we're less than or behind. It's not a cliché like a New Year's resolution. This is a serious investment in our present and future. Avoiding our brokenness will cost us more down the road, while investing in our breakthrough will grant us more in the long run.

Building Back Better

We must first address the root of the problem at hand or any surface additions and supplemental repairs will be done in vain. Whether it's the one with Chip and Joanna or Scott and Drew, every home repair show encounters a costly, unseen repair such as additional support beams, updated wiring and electric, or busted water pipes. And you'll hear the phrase "No one likes spending money where you can't see it, but I promise this will be well worth the investment."

I get it! It's not glamorous to do the inner work. There's a reason retail therapy is prized and true therapy is shied away from. You can buy a cute top and show it off on the same day, but a new heart takes time and grit. If you're navigating heartbreak, the widely accepted and supposedly gratifying medicine is to go on a rebound date, hit the town with your friends, or take that perfect photo to make your ex jealous . . . well, if he's still following you on Instagram, which you now have to check right away and— STOP!

It doesn't work.

What seems too good to be true often is. The advertised "quick fix" doesn't truly *fix* much. There's a reason some journeys are referred to as the "path of least resistance." Healing takes time and determination, just like building a home. I've learned that lesson both personally and professionally. I reference homes as examples because I love designing and flipping them. (Hey, HGTV, if you need a new show, I'll keep my phone nearby!) But quicker and easier isn't always better or longer-lasting, especially in our shelters—be it our hearts or our homes.

When my husband, Arden, and I flipped our first property in Nashville—a cozy brick loft downtown—we did it all ourselves by removing what wasn't working in the space's favor and building a better design, but quickly. Time is money in renovation! One of the biggest upgrades was the kitchen, where we added a stunning island, open shelving, and a Calacatta marble backsplash. When we bought the beautiful Italian stone, the store associate told us about a new time-saving backsplash application that was much quicker and easier than traditional grout. Basically, it was a lay-and-stick method—um, yes, give me that versus hours of mixing messy sand-like material. We spent a few hours laying the tile, and it was stunning—one of my favorite backsplash looks! The next day we returned to the property and found the kitchen floor covered in pieces of what was supposed to be our beautiful back-splash. Overnight, the dream solution turned into a nightmare. We had to rebuy all the materials and start over, this time using grout. Lesson learned.

At the end of the day, the quick and easy route proved futile and doubled the work. Now we *always* go with the proven, long-lasting method, even if it does require more work. Because we've seen firsthand that the outcome is worth it. Trying to heal broken areas of our lives with easy fixes will just lead to more brokenness.

I remember taking that familiar route after every high school or college breakup and only ever feeling spent afterward. I'd bury all my emotions, letdowns, and frustrations and hope I could turn the corner to something comforting. But those emotions were building up like bursting water pipes. We can only shove so much down before we bust.

After my last breakup, I was ready to accept that my system of dealing with heartbreak—along with my insecurities, afflictions, and self-reproach—was broken, and it stemmed from somewhere deep and affected others in my life (more on that later). I knew at least one brick was loose, and I didn't want everything to come crumbling down. It was time for me to pay a pretty penny, roll up my sleeves, and assess the damage.

Many of us would have no clue where to begin if our actual home's foundation started to crack. We'd need to call a professional. I felt that way with my heart. This was work for someone who knew what they were doing, who knew the infrastructure inside and out. So, on a rainy Friday night, with zero plans but numerous emotions, I plopped down on my bedroom floor and said, "God, I'm a mess. I need you to teach me how to heal from the inside out."

Trying to heal broken areas of our lives with easy fixes will just lead to more brokenness.

That admittance signaled a new beginning. A chance for freedom from the downhill spiral I'd been in. It freed me from the internal prison I'd been keeping myself in. Ironically, the more I accepted and admitted, the more I felt acquitted. Now, I find no pleasure in starting a "Yay, We're All Hot Messes" club. The movie rights to that story have already been taken anyways. But I do hope that through this book, you'll find that any brokenness you've experienced is not your end but your beginning.

When we fall, we have a Father who's willing to pick us up and dust us off. He shows us a new way, a better way. When we turn to Him and raise our hands in that childlike posture of surrender, He's able to lift us up to where we long to be. But we must adopt that position of surrender and trust His plan. After all, as our Creator, He knows the layout for our lives best. As Psalm 127:1 says, "Unless the Lord builds the house, the builders labor in vain."

This verse puts it plainly: we *need* God. He is our firm foundation for every area of life. We see this truth repeated throughout Scripture:

- "Behold, I am the one who has laid as a foundation in Zion, a stone, a tested stone, a precious cornerstone, of a sure foundation: 'Whoever believes will not be in haste'" (Isa. 28:16 ESV).
- "He is like a man building a house, who dug deep and laid the foundation on the rock. And when a flood arose, the stream broke against that house and could not shake it, because it had been well built" (Luke 6:48 ESV).
- "According to the grace of God given to me, like a skilled master builder I laid a foundation, and someone else is building upon it. Let each one take care how he builds upon it" (1 Cor. 3:10 ESV).
- "Christ Jesus himself being the cornerstone" (Eph. 2:20 ESV).

Jesus is the Master; He can find the cracks we've been covering and identify the source of the decay. In my semidefeated state, crying out to God for guidance, I knew I had plenty of good intentions in my search for love. But from my track record, it was evident I was not qualified to handle my relationships on my own. I also knew this area was tied to my self-esteem, my mental health, and my faith. Once I was honest in my self-assessment, I concluded that on my own I was unskilled in the art of developing feelings, illiterate in reading my own motives, and inexperienced in fostering a healthy approach to conflict. It was time to call in the professional. He came in and allowed what could have crumbled to be built back better.

Famous for What's Breaking

In the last year, I've been shocked to see ghastly and heartbreaking statements spread across social media platforms. In the rise of the debate around abortion, men and women alike went so far as to say they wished their own mothers had aborted them because they despised their lives. Despite the feminist movement claiming to unite females everywhere, women are tearing each other apart more than ever in comment threads, shaming one another for how they look or what they believe. Our generation has seen isolation and failing mental health lead many to lost relationships, stolen peace, and most heartbreaking of all, the devaluing of life and purpose.

We haven't been rebuilding from our breakage, we've been burying. Currently we're facing terrifying facts like these:

- 73 percent of Gen Z report they feel alone either sometimes or always.
- Gen Z's mental health is at risk, with only 45 percent reporting "excellent" or "very good" mental health—the lowest of any generation.[1]
- Nearly half of Gen Z and millennials globally say they are stressed all or most of the time.[2]

Could it be that we feel broken because we're not standing on a firm foundation? In tough times, especially, we need solid ground.

The Leaning Tower of Pisa has become famous for its slope. But what caused the slant in the first place? The ground underneath the structure is unstable. Over decades, it's been giving way on one side, causing an increasing degree of lean.[3] It's not just London Bridge that's falling down!

Many of us have seen a Facebook friend's tourist photo reenacting the signature "Pisa pose" with their hands up as if they're supporting the famous structure from falling over. While there are numerous fascinating buildings across Italy still standing strong today, travelers prefer to pay good money to see one that's sinking. Like the fascination with the precarious Italian bell tower's slope, I've seen a societal tolerance of personal breakage. People pose beside the building, ignoring the potential danger with a smile, and sometimes I think we do the same when our lives are crumbling at the foundation. It's almost as if we're taking selfies with our pain points without acknowledging the true impending danger they pose.

Shifting soil can cause a landslide. Pisa sits off-kilter today because what's underneath couldn't stand the test of time. Let's not make the same mistake with our souls. I applaud anyone who has the courage to come forth in an area of struggle and say, "I need help" or "This is the journey I'm on, but I know it's not my end." What's been off-kilter in your life can be recalibrated with Christ. But first, you have to identify what's been breaking you down.

We have faulty foundations to address. We have structures to secure. If we forsake the rebuilding process, we risk our own health and put those around us in harm's way. Take these chapters to heart and notice how each one speaks to your life.

We've All Been Broken

I'm not shy about the fact that I married a great man. He's faithful, attractive, courageous, dependable . . . I could go on. But what surprised me after we got married was the recurring question I'd get from other women. No, not "Does he have a brother?!" (I knew that one was inevitable.) I was shocked by how often someone asked me what I did to get a great guy like Arden. Was there some secret formula? Each time I'd respond, "Everything wrong."

It's true. I stumbled and strayed more than I'd like to admit while navigating singleness. I didn't "deserve" an incredible man or a wonderful marriage because of anything I'd done. And beyond that, my husband wasn't a trophy I'd won.

Granted, I do feel like a winner being with him, but I didn't beat out the competition by being some elite and worthy contestant. I didn't put in a certain number of hours at my local charity or have a squeaky-clean halo to coerce God's favor. But I did have flaws that were met with God's overabundant grace.

We are not perfect, and blessings are not prizes.

See, in relationships, and life in general, we believe we must be pristine and we'll be rewarded. But that's just not how this whole thing works—*thank goodness*. This should be a relief to everyone reading this, because only one person was ever able to do this life without fault. That same person now sits at the right hand of God advocating for His truth and power to take root in our lives—not through our works but through His grace.

We are not perfect, and blessings are not prizes.

Christ Himself is the avenue that allows us to receive the gifts of God. James 1:17 states that "every good and perfect gift is from above." Notice the use of the word *gift* over *prize* or *reward*. Any fruit we yield or praiseworthy portion we exhibit begins and ends with His goodness, not our own. Every blessing is God's glory on display, freely given apart from our own deservingness attached.

I think somewhere in our human attempt at being good, we made the course jagged. As a kid, we may have been told that if we were on our best behavior, we could get a treat after dinner. Or perhaps if we acted out, instead of dealing with the issue at hand, we lost the privilege of playing with a toy or watching TV. When we're young, we need direction and guidance to teach us as we grow in our character and understanding. But we're not robots—we err because our minds, emotions, and feelings are not systematic. When a child makes a mistake, it's an opportunity to learn *why* it was incorrect and *how* to do better. The same is true in our spiritual walk.

God never asks His children to be perfect. Instead, He asks for our hearts and obedience—instruments through which He gives us wisdom and guidance. What we commonly misunderstand as a need for perfection is actually an invitation to righteousness—to be in right standing with Christ. No one gets to that place on their own; it happens only through relationship with God. His atonement allows us to draw near to Him and resemble Him as we are influenced by His majesty.

The Bible says *He* makes us spotless—as white as snow. From as far as the east is from the west, that's how far who we have been, and what we have done, is separated from who we are in Him (Ps. 103:12). Redemption severs our ties to any brokenness caused by regret, anxiety, shame, comparison, self-deprecation—all of which we'll work through in this book—and offers us a path to breakthrough with a promise of blessed belonging. No matter what we feel inside right now, no one is disinvited from this invitation.

Surveying the Bible, we see those who were once disgraced display the goodness of God. He chose to use murderers, adulterers, the forgotten, shameful, unqualified, prideful, scandalous, and guilty for His glory. Here's a liberating truth bomb: you and I are imperfect beings, incapable of righting our own wrongs. Yet, through the gift of grace, He leads us from broken to beloved. For we were all broken before Christ—every single one of us. Not a single exemplary figure in the Bible was exempt from some type of failure, nor would they have been notable on their own—they depended on His grace and mercy, as we all do. There's no moral or righteous claim to fame that does not begin or end with God.

When we walk with Him, we experience far better and greater than we could ever achieve or imagine! I didn't "get" anything in life as a prize for being good enough or by lucky chance. I've seen an abundance of God's goodness—both in the joy of the highs and in the strengthening of the lows—when I put my full trust and confidence in Him. Both the blessings and blessings in disguise are results of following and trusting that God's Word is true, a trusty compass.

I was skeptical at first too. I thought I'd blown it in nearly every area, that the brokenness I felt deep down inside would follow me forever. If it had been possible to foresee all God was going to do in my life in the last five years alone, I would have been the first to call a bluff on it all. "There's no way," I would have challenged. Surely I had broken His heart with my callous disregard for His instruction one too many times. I was a fraction of who I "should" have been. That pristine daughter He deserved was chipped and crushed, better off left behind.

Not on His watch.

In an instant, God can redirect us from the faulty path we've been on and set us back on course. Paul can attest to that! On the road to Damascus, his entire life changed through breaking down before Christ—being blinded by seeing the glory in His presence. In a matter of three days, Paul went from persecuting Christians to being healed and baptized by one. The account states that in the latter moment something like scales fell from his eyes when he received his sight. I believe that's significant to how veiled he'd been to the truth. When Jesus meets you face-to-face on your own dusty road of deception, it's nearly impossible to remain the same. The encounter transforms you.

Your brokenness doesn't define you when Christ defends you.

God has a breakthrough waiting for you, His beloved. But much like Paul, you must turn from where you were headed. I meant what I said earlier—God can do far more with the real you than the false image you hide behind. He can take your broken heart and make it whole. He can take your broken hopes and give them a second chance. He can take your broken name and fashion you a new one.

Your brokenness doesn't define you when Christ defends you.

His bold love steps in where we've been lacking and sets out with us on the escapade of redemption. Where we see imperfections, His perfect love makes the correction. Where we've fallen short, His mercy creates a safety net. His plans for us don't stop at the first sign of damage; they start a new road to restoration. If you feel like you're broken down on the side of the road, lost, or turned around, let Him lead you down this new road. Trust the journey and the destination.

A big catalyst for writing this book was to correct how we view ourselves in brokenness and blessings. I hope no other woman ever asks me what I did to get blessed; instead, I hope she wants to know what I'm doing with my blessing. You may also be blessed with an exemplary spouse or a career that pays the bills and fills you up or a houseful of children or an ailment that healed miraculously. Every one of us has been entrusted with blessings we can either take for granted or make an impact with. The blessing we all have is the gift of a second chance—for our redemption and God's repurposing. God offers that to you freely, but before you can wholeheartedly take His hand, you must let go of what you're still holding on to. You need to break up with what broke you.

Leaving Your Less for More

Breakups are typically synonymous with rocky road ice cream, rom-com reruns, and rough crying sessions. They mean heartache and suggest individual brokenness. But what if the breakup isn't the cause of pain, but instead is the liberation you've needed? A good breakup can set you loose from a bad love affair. It can void the chains that bound you to a broken system. A toxic relationship is a festering ground for regret. A clean break is a chance for healing.

Some breakups in life and in fiction are memorable because they show how we can be better off taking that leap of faith than we are staying in the wrong relationship. For example, Rachel dumping Ross on *Friends* after he cheated because they were definitely *not* on a break. (Some will disagree with me here, but I'm okay with that.) Or perhaps whomever Beyoncé was singing about in the power hit "Irreplaceable," telling that guy to the left, to the left. Some breakups are needed so we can find the right thing— whether that's the right partner or, more keenly related to this book, the right path.

You must break up with what broke you to find your breakthrough. You can leave your less for more. You can stop settling and start succeeding. These are what I like to call "For the Best" breakups.

The Benefits of a "For the Best" Breakup

1. Severance from your past
2. Ability to grow from mistakes
3. Flourishing in your mental health
4. Creating unshakable confidence
5. Cultivating healthier relationships
6. Developing intimacy with God
7. Replacing bad habits with better ones
8. Gaining a mindset marked by peace

It's time to say sayonara and good riddance to your inner inclination toward negativity. You've gotta break up with that inner critic bringing you down. And I mean a clean break! Burn the old photos that bring back painful memories, throw out the old sweater that reminds you of shame, block the calls of regret that won't leave you alone. Breaking up with what broke you will be the most liberating, transformative split you'll ever have.

Promise me, and yourself, that over the next chapters you'll take each page to heart. My goal is to become your literary "best friend" who tells you the truth, even when it's hard, like your real-life best friend who wouldn't let you get back with your bad-news ex. When it comes to the hurts and hindrances of the past, change your number, throw out the keys, and pack those bags, baby, because your breakthrough journey starts now!

02. Broken Moments We Can't Forget

There was a long hard time when I kept far from me the re-
membrance of what I had thrown away when I was quite igno-
rant of its worth.

—Charles Dickens

There are moments that feel like they last a lifetime—our first kiss, a difficult goodbye, looking in the rearview mirror right before a car crash. Seconds can become scenes locked into our memories. These moments happen almost in slow-motion. That's because even though it takes one hundred milliseconds to create a moment, the psychological effects of that moment can last a lifetime. When a memory is positive, these effects are marvelous. But when that moment was a breaking point, they can be haunting.

Professor of psychiatry J. Kim Penberthy wrote an article on how regret connects to our psyche. She states that imaging studies reveal that feelings of regret show increased activity in an area of the brain involved in decision-making called the medial orbito-frontal cortex. Essentially, our feelings or moments of regret aren't reserved to our actions in the past but influence the decisions we make, ways we behave, and what we believe about our future.[1]

For example, if you were learning an activity like snowboarding and crashed, your instructor may check on you, then tell you to get up and try again. People use this tactic to help one quickly get back to accomplishing the task at hand and not let negative emotions or memories set in. How we carry and remember events in our lives has a major influence on our mental state, perception, and even happiness.

In her article, Penberthy also states that dealing with regret is exceedingly difficult because it can bring on other secondary emotions, such as remorse, sorrow, and helplessness. "Regret can increase our stress, negatively affect physical health and throw off the balance of hormone and immune systems. Regret is not only unpleasant. It is unhealthy."[2]

Whoever you are and wherever you've come from, you likely have that one moment you wish you could forget. *That moment everything shifted.* You know—the one that lingers, whispering nasty lies from the back seat and taking you off course every now and then. That moment when perhaps, tragically, your innocence was stolen, false identities were formed, trust was broken, lust was awakened. Something occurred that introduced the feeling of *brokenness* for the first time. We must break up with the moments we regret so we can see clearly who we're becoming.

Pinpoint the Moment

The first step in breaking up with the moments we regret is to pinpoint the moment(s). This is the memory that interrupts our purpose and tries to lead us astray by tying us to something ugly in the past. It's the time we regret, the event we can't stand to remember, or the instance we don't speak of, not even to our best friends. It happens so fast but leaves so slowly.

Is there a specific moment you're thinking of now? Maybe something was taken, you were misled, or you made a rash decision. It could be that you started watching pornography, casually hooking up, or running with the wrong crowd. Let me go ahead and tell you now—that moment is *not* the one that defines you. But you must identify these moments so that they don't hold you hostage.

If you've ever broken a bone or sustained a major injury, one of the first questions you're asked is "What happened?" Pain can be eliminated and healing expedited if your medical team knows where and how the damage occurred. We can take this same principle and apply it to our lives. We can't know how to heal until we know what needs healing. Identify where your regret could be stemming from. What areas of your life are hard to deal with, difficult to relive, or cause you to take one step forward then two steps back?

If we let these moments of regret define us, we allow a broken record of lies to play on repeat. Think about it, what emotions arise when you recollect that moment now? Regret whispers deprecating ideas and paints a picture in which we see ourselves as screwups, victims, or fragments of who we'd hoped to be. It aims to twist our identity and take away from our future. If you've battled these tall tales and feel stuck in a loop of "oh no" or "oh well," I want to interject some powerful truth that will change the way you recall these moments and how you move forward toward your future.

Let's use this chapter to repurpose, restore, and resurrect the moment(s) that left you feeling broken. Trade any skepticism about your future, all anxiety from your past, and/or your hesitation to leave it all behind for a fixed confidence that there is better ahead.

If I Had Only Known

In my research and conversations for this book, *everyone* admitted that we don't plan these moments. We don't set out to become "that girl" at the party, to become addicted or anxious or part of the crowd we used to avoid. But when we do realize we've carried heavy burdens or are discontented with where we are, we can see that somewhere along the road, we took a wrong turn. These wrong turns are often rooted in a misconception, pain point, or past trauma that was unaddressed or overlooked.

This book is about breaking up with anything that has broken or attempts to break us, not just relationship breakups. For some of us, those breakups have been our breaking point. I know that was true for me. My haunting moment crept up so sneakily that I didn't see it coming (or chose not to), and it happened so fast that I looked back and thought, *How did I get here?*

Have you ever asked yourself that same question?

Growing up, I thought boys were more fun to play sports with than to fool around with. I remember telling God that I should be a nun when I grew up. Bless the women who do follow such a path, but it's a safe bet that my husband's glad God had other plans for me. So what changed? How did I go from wanting to live in a nunnery to a relationship being a breaking point for me?

I wondered the same thing, but it wasn't until a few years ago that I began to piece together how my thoughts and desires had morphed and what had caused them to do so.

My parents separated when I was very young, and my whole understanding of love and intimacy was a bit muddled. I understood virginity, but sex was foreign. I got the point of *The Scarlet Letter* but neglected Song of Solomon. My parents were intentional about teaching me strong morals, including that my virginity was a precious gift and sex was saved for marriage—both true and great to teach your children! Even still, there's truth to the notion that a vital part of learning is experience. I heard every word they said, but without the experience of seeing a husband and wife's relationship dynamic up close, I felt I knew the formula of an equation without understanding the solution. I grew to believe that virginity = good, and sex = bad.

This belief was further solidified by well-intended but overly intense purity messages I heard during youth nights at church. Especially in the Southern Bible Belt, the understanding around intimacy can easily become twisted. Even still, I believed my virginity was a gift and wanted to save that precious part of myself for the man I'd one day marry.

Let me go ahead and pause here to break down that half-truth for anyone who's currently where I was in that thinking—sex is *not* a sin or a weapon. It's a physical, emotional, and spiritual instrument of intimacy from God that's a vital component in connecting husband and wife. Sex is good! But sex is also passion, and passion is a fire. In a safe, controlled environment, it can provide sustenance for two people; however, when lit carelessly and allowed to burn rampant, fire can tarnish and scorch. When we put a label on something so valuable, we can make young girls afraid of intimacy, or in withholding the truth that sex is good within God's intention for it, we can awaken an eagerness in some to prematurely find out just *how* good it is.

When I started high school, I was astonished by how many of my friends and schoolmates were already having sex. I thought, *If this many people are doing it, am I missing something?* One day, as a girlfriend and I were daydreaming about finding "the one," we both shared our ideal checklist. I blushed as I dreamt about my future husband: *tall, handsome, athletic, kind, and pure.* My soulmate was somewhere out there, I just knew it! I began to share what I had written, and as I studied my friend's face, my daydreams were swept away like a dark cloud. I went over what I had listed. *Okay, maybe tall isn't necessarily essential,* I thought. Surely that was the only thing that could have been wrong with what I had written.

She looked me straight in the eyes and said, "No guy is saving himself for marriage. You need to lower your standards if you ever want to meet someone." Almost ten years later, I can still remember that moment like it was yesterday.

I felt exposed and embarrassed. My heart sank. *Stupid, naive me for thinking guys were like that.* What she said had to be true. I mean, the guys at our school weren't saving themselves. And if my girlfriends didn't share my beliefs, how on earth could I find a guy who did?

That day struck a chord in my belief system. I decided that since they were becoming a rarity, instead of looking for a guy who was a virgin, I would just be one for him. Sure! I mean, it was *my* virginity that was the gift, right? It didn't matter if he wasn't saving himself for me. I just needed to save myself. I'd made a promise to God. I could keep my word and still find love—it was a win-win. The only thing I didn't realize about that philosophy was that if you dated a guy who had already had sex, unless he had adopted a new belief, after a while he'd want you to do the same with him.

I began dating and realized that no matter how much a guy said he *loved* that I was saving myself and respected my decision, he had a secretly ticking clock. If I didn't give in before time was up, he'd give up. I didn't know whether to be frustrated with the guy for making it such a priority or with myself for playing such an obvious losing game. *What am I waiting for? No one else is saving themselves.* I got nothing but picked on for not wanting to have sex until I was married. Frustration and embarrassment rose up like a wave and drowned every good intention I had. I could feel my hopes for a healthy marriage and urge to live a pure life crushing under the weight of my desires for immediate love and acceptance. Something dangerous was stirring within me: disbelief. I hadn't given in to the act with my body, but my heart began to buy into the idea that to find love, I had to lose myself. I'd find myself thinking, *What's so special about waiting? Will someone think I'm special if I do?*

Many times, our brokenness originates within a broken belief.

This is what we must realize—the world is not a reliable source to build our beliefs on. If we take the Bible at its word, it says the dominion of the world is infiltrated with the enemy's tactics. He will try to get us to doubt what we believe and pull us away from

Many times, our brokenness originates within a broken belief.

what God has in store for us. I knew God's Word, and I knew His plan for marriage. But when the enemy came to steal, kill, and destroy, I inclined my ear to what the world was saying more than I meditated on what God had said. The enemy is a liar, but his timing is impeccable.

Broken Promises

Frustrated, isolated, and desperate for love, I was all ears to the lies. "Someone just love me," my soul cried out. I fell head over heels for a guy I thought was one of a kind. I say head over heels because everything except my head was leading me into that relationship. He was handsome, talented, kind, tall, and most of all, alluring. As we started seeing each other, I realized we had differing views and goals. His lifestyle was not one I envisioned for my future, and I knew that in a few months I would be transferring to a university hours away. It didn't make sense to date, but his eyes were an ocean I was ready to dive into. Looking back now I can see that I loved the idea of loving him more than I was committed to loving myself through God's lens.

In any relationship, the more emotionally intimate you become with someone, the more intimacy you begin to crave with them in other areas. That's why dating should be a time not for exploration but for examination. *(Adding that to the list of things I wish I could have told my younger self.)* After months of dating, he wanted more, and I didn't want to lose him or my chance at finally being loved . . . so I gave in.

The moment I referred to earlier, the one that brings us to our knees and breaks us down—this was mine. Afterward, I tucked my head in defeat, hoping that what had just happened was somehow a figment of my imagination. As tears began to roll down my cheeks, I realized it wasn't.

All I could do was sit and cry.

Have you ever found yourself in a similar state? When you realize you've lost hope, it can cause a flood of emotions. The years

I'd spent preparing for my future marriage seemed to have been swept away by a single instance, like a wave washing over what I'd written in the sand—making it fleeting and forgotten. I felt like a disappointment. I'd broken my promise—to God, to my future husband, to myself.

I know abstinence is debated as merely a religious discipline these days. But let me be clear that the pain I felt wasn't simply from "messing up" physically but from the realization that I had become so scared to be let down in what I was believing that I let my guard down instead. The tears were from the little girl inside of me who went off course in search of love but didn't find a treasure box when she handed over the keys.

Whenever you break a promise, cross a line, or let yourself or someone else down, regret will take the empty seat hope once occupied. It doesn't care if it's welcome or not; it just makes itself at home in your moment of distress.

I began to flash back over my former conversations and choices, tracing the cause-and-effect trail that had led me there. *How did I let myself get so off track? How did I not realize where I was headed? Why did I let others' lack of hope for what I believed steal all of mine?* In that moment when I gave in, the devil succeeded in *stealing* my focus from God's blessings, *killing* my confidence in my worth and virtue, and *destroying* how I saw myself.

But again, I hadn't *intended* to be there. I was looking for love, trying to find myself and be true to what I felt. That's what we're all trying to do, right? We're designed to be in relationships and we're built for connection. But where I went wrong was when I fully embraced the false reality of all the lies and half-truths I had been told up to that point. In turn, I lacked vision for God's promises. Sometimes the doors we leave open wreak havoc on our good intentions and strong beliefs, even when they're cracked ever so slightly.

When all feels heavy or lost, we have a choice in how we respond: *flight* or *fight*. Flight looks like avoidance, blame, wallowing, rebellion, or withdrawal. It often buries the pain and slaps some duct tape on the breakage. It's not a positive or permanent response to what we've been through. I chose flight for a long time, and my regret only grew deeper while remaining hidden beneath the surface. Fighting, however, looks like acknowledging, uncovering, struggling, growing, and healing. It means coming to terms with our faults and mistakes, releasing regret through repentance, and beginning a new hope journey.

Grammatically, there's one small difference in these responses, and there's one huge difference in how we pick which route we follow. A single L separates these two words, and the single act of *love* changes their outcomes. I realized that love—true, authentic love—was what I had been missing all along.

I wasn't loving God, my future husband, or myself with my body. Instead, I was operating out of fear. I was so scared of giving myself away for a false form of love, disappointing God, and feeling inadequate that I eventually made those very things happen. That's why they say you can't just run *from* something; you need to run *to* something.

I broke my promises because I was operating from a broken place—fear. Fear whispers anxieties and doubts that cloud our judgment and make us run through life like we're trying to find our way out of a corn maze. But we don't need to frantically look for a way out; we need a clear direction for where we're going. What can provide that? Love. The Word tells us that perfect love casts out fear (1 John 4:18). As God healed my heart, I learned that love needed to be my driving force. Because I loved God, I'd keep His commandments (5:3). Because I loved my future husband, I'd wait for him. Because I loved myself, I'd value my heart and body.

I contrast that moment of weeping from regret with weeping while I walked down the aisle on my wedding day. I had believed my friend when she said I'd never meet a virgin, yet there I was about to marry a man who had saved himself for me. I believed that any guy I dated would eventually just want me to have sex with him, but at that moment I was facing a man who not only respected my purity but fought for it. If only I had truly believed what I knew to be true. If only I had talked through my disbelief and exposed the lies for what they were. If only I had known how dirty the devil plays against us.

There are no do-overs in life, but there is redemption.

When I think back to how I stumbled, I'm grateful for a God who saves. At no point in my brokenness was God's Word broken. "If we are faithless, He remains faithful [true to His word and His righteous character], for He cannot deny Himself" (2 Tim. 2:13 AMP). He always had that man of purity waiting on me. He always had plans for a healthy family for me. I was able to still have hope once repentance released my regret, because all along hope was not lost; it was simply out of view. God never lets us down, even when we let ourselves down.

There are no do-overs in life, but there is redemption.

The enemy's snare is in making us think we're too far gone, that we've been on this road too long and turning back would be nearly impossible. I'm here to tell you the truth—it's just another lie! A single step in the direction of healing can offer more freedom than the ten thousand prior ones. "For my yoke is easy and my burden is light" (Matt. 11:30). I plead with you to turn around and go back to what you know to be true. I give you my word that you won't regret it.

I can only imagine how much it hurt God's heart to see me go down paths I was never meant to travel. Paths He knew would bring me pain while He wanted to lead me to a hope and a future. Part of God's sovereign splendor is that though He makes a clear path for us, He's never thrown off when we take a wrong turn. It doesn't matter how lost we find ourselves or how far off track we've gone, as soon as we give Him control back, He puts us on the right course. Like the prodigal son in Luke 15, He meets the return of His beloved with open arms. Though we are aware of our faults and proclaim we are no longer worthy to be His, He celebrates our homecoming by lavishing grace on us and dressing us in honor. Our Father doesn't keep us at arm's length, He wraps us completely in a warm embrace.

Will we let go of those moments that hold us back so we can run back to Him?

Leave the Past in the Past

There have been recent pushes to hire more females in various work fields. One employer that could significantly benefit from more women is the FBI. How? Have you not seen the speed and accuracy with which a female can discover a potential date's red flags or bad history with one Facebook search? Or how meticulously a girl can keep tabs on her ex after a breakup? We're special agents already; just give us five minutes with a cell phone, and we'll have the dirt on your suspect pronto, 10-4?!

I'm not proud to admit that I've done what many of us have done after a breakup—social media stalked. Yep, I've searched their recently followed accounts or posted a photo and checked to see if they "liked" it. I may have even made a fake Instagram account once, but I cannot confirm or deny that. Why do we women put ourselves through these tireless, needless games, letting someone who hurt us only hurt us further after the fact?

Helpful tip: your ex will move on at some point. The only people benefiting from your obsessing over old photos and searching their pages are the folks at Ben & Jerry's. Inevitably, doing so just makes you upset and causes you to reach for that comfort pint of ice cream. In the end, you'll end up regretting the time you spent overthinking.

The same is true for our breakup with regret. We must leave the past in the past. I know it can be hard to forget the moments that caused us pain, but it's necessary for our healing. Wishing for do-overs is impossible and unprofitable. Part of the human condition is that we will err, but we can learn from our errors. We cannot be active in our future if we've cemented our feet in the past.

There's a rom-com titled *About Time* in which the protagonist time travels, allowing him to correct mistakes and get do-overs whenever he needs one. He inherits this ability from his father, who, as he approaches the end of his life, shares his secret formula for happiness with his son. What do you think he says? "Get rid of every regretful moment!" That's what we'd assume. Instead, he tells his son to live each day normally. Then at the end of each day, go back and relive it a second time without changing a thing except how you perceive it. This line in the monologue captures the notion beautifully: "[Live] the first time with all the tensions and worries that stop us noticing how sweet the world can be, but the second time noticing."[3]

If we stay in the past, we miss out on the present and, in turn, the future. I imagine our Heavenly Father, the only One not confined to time, would give us the same advice as the father in the movie. See the beauty in the now. Untether yourself from the past. Acknowledge that traveling back in time is only possible in cinema, but you're able to better your future now. Accepting the gift of God's grace and mercy, you can move in the direction He has created for you content and with expectation.

Acknowledge the Pain

There's something powerful in acknowledging what has hurt us or our hopes and untethering ourselves from it.

I shared my broken moment with you in the hope that it can help you see that we all have moments we wish we could change. And as we release them, we also release the power they hold over us. Perhaps your moment is different from mine, or you need more convincing that change is possible. During my lowest moments, I'm often comforted by how God uses imperfect, dare I say broken, people to showcase His glory and redemption in His Word.

The Bible is full of testimonies of radical change, many of which I'll share in the coming chapters. Because what's more encouraging than reading how God used the flawed flawlessly? Question: When it comes to replacing regret, which story would encourage you more: one about a Canaanite prostitute or Jesus's heroic great(x31)-grandmother? Well, depending on which moment in the narrative you're referencing, Rahab was both.

When Joshua set out to conquer Jericho, he sent two spies to survey the land. On their mission, they sought refuge in Rahab's home. She lived on the poor outskirts of town where she was known as a prostitute. The king of Jericho, informed of an invasion, sent her a message telling her there were two spies in her home and she had to turn them over. Instead of complying, she hid the men on her rooftop and sent the king's messengers on a wild goose chase.

I find Rahab's actions completely contradictory from expectation. A native of the land who was used to being objectified by men stuck her neck out for two strangers. Now, there's no telling what led Rahab to prostitution in the first place. The dire need for food or shelter is a likely reason, but I cannot imagine how she felt in the moment she first gave over her body. Did her family push her to do it so that she could provide for them? Or did someone take advantage of her? Either way, we can assume how difficult it must have been to forsake any security she had earned for two men she didn't know. *Why* would she do such a thing? And equally important, *how* could she do such a thing?

How she was able to act unstirred by the consequences of the law means she must have had a strong *why*. Joshua 2 shares Rahab's leading motivation. She told the spies that the Lord had given their people this land and that by His mighty works her people trembled: "For the LORD your God is God in heaven above and on the earth below" (v. 11). What Rahab believed about these men and God was bigger than what she believed about her land, her risks, and herself.

To break up with what broke you, you'll need your own strong why. Sometimes there are personal whys: You may want a lasting marriage and to raise your kids in a healthy home even though you didn't experience either. Or you may want to overcome your insecurities and obstacles to make your parents proud. These are compelling, proficient whys, but I challenge you to make your first why focused on the Creator. I imagine Rahab wanted more for her life, for her family, and for her future. But the stories of God's supremacy were what ultimately moved her to the point of action. We may *want* more for our life, but we *need* more of God.

We can only help, motivate, and rehabilitate ourselves so far, then comes Christ. He is the ultimate why, the divine restorer, the caring Savior who redeems our moments of regret and creates in us moments to shine His glory.

So what happened next in the story? Rahab helped the two spies escape by lowering a scarlet cord from her window so they could sneak past their pursuers. Because of her kindness, they promised that if she tied a scarlet cord in her window as a signal, she and her family would be spared when they conquered the city. In that moment, the entire trajectory of Rahab's life changed. She went from being bound by a scarlet letter life to having the chance of a new life through a scarlet cord.

Joshua and his army claimed Canaan, spared Rahab's family, and accepted them into their tribe. She went on to marry Salmon and give birth to another person whose name you might recognize: Boaz. The course, purpose, and benefactors of her life were changed by a single moment resulting from a strong why.

Like Rahab, I saw that when I put my trust in God—need I mention my *full* trust in Him—He cleaned out my dirty closet better than Marie Kondo and led me to a husband and family far better than I could have imagined. I'm not saying my son, Azariah, is the next Boaz, but the kid is seriously cute. It still baffles me that my life is so starkly different from how it could have been. That's how powerful our moments and our whys are. I'm always moved by Rahab's story because it shows that anyone anywhere can change in an instant, and God is more concerned with your future than your past. It validates the transformation process for you and me. A single moment can throw us off course, yet a single moment can also correct our purpose.

Friend, the lies you've believed do not define you. Maybe you've believed the lie that your moment(s) has in some way altered who you can be or where you are going. As believers, we need to adjust how we view cause and effect. Normally, as I did, we think if we have failed, we are failures. If we squander our virginity, we are no longer wholesome. If we go down the wrong road, there's no turning back. But the truth is, we are defined not by what we've done but rather by what Christ has done for us.

Friend, the lies you've believed do not define you.

It was painful to encounter my own brokenness and know there was nothing I could do. But for every ounce of brokenness I felt, God was ready to match it with redemption. In my own strength, I couldn't remove the pain or regret from my story or my memories. When I stopped trying in my own might to fix myself and offered my pain, frustration, and remorse to God, the miraculous happened. If God is not limited to time or space, why would He be limited to what we understand as possible? In my might, it was impossible to make that gift what it once was. But not in God's. Redemption supersedes recklessness. The tainted feeling I'd carried for far too long needed to be extracted, and only He could perform such a surgery. In essence, His grace was sufficient for me, for His power was made perfect in my weakness or brokenness (2 Cor. 12:9–11). He alone is mighty to redeem.

Which moment will you let define you? Will you be audacious enough to believe there's a new, better chapter ahead of you? Will you believe your future shines brighter than your past and God has called you by name to be His? Don't let who you've been discredit who you're called to be. If He can do it for Rahab, He can do it for you too—*if* you let Him.

We cannot change the past, but we can alter how we perceive it. The visible and psychological damage that happened can be swept away by *one moment* of the Father's love. I fully believe God wants to repurpose, restore, and resurrect any area or moment we offer up to Him. I'm thankful that God turned me around from where I was going and put me back on course. He repurposed my hope, restored my purity, and resurrected my desire for a healthy marriage.

As we rely on God, we are made new (2 Cor. 5:17). Where we were once deceived or fragile, we can become unyielding and resilient. We will never graduate from our reliance on God, but as believers we must stand firm in our faith despite anything that comes against us. I know I never again want to be deceived because I wasn't standing firm in my faith.

I said at the beginning of this chapter that the moment that defines you is not the moment of regret—it's the moment on the cross. Jesus's sacrifice covered a multitude of sins, including those you did out of weakness and those committed against you. We must believe redemption is waiting for us and Someone who loves us with such strength is stronger than what led to brokenness.

To break up with regret, you need to:

1. Pinpoint the moment.
2. Leave the past in the past.
3. Acknowledge the pain.

As you put these three practices into motion, I pray regret dissipates from your life and each step loosens that white-knuckle grasp you have on the past, bringing you closer to an openhanded release to God. One moment you'll never regret is going all in with Him.

03. Anxiety Monsters

There is nothing like suspense and anxiety for barricading a human's mind against [God].

—C. S. Lewis

I remember the nights I lay awake in bed as a child, convinced a big green monster with beady eyes and a nasty growl was lurking under my bed. I'd imagine that it had crawled under there when no one was looking and was waiting for the perfect opportunity to pounce—when I was alone and in the dark. Riddled with fear, I'd seek some sense of protection or peace. I convinced myself that my bed—a tiny twin-size mattress—was my safe zone, and my thin princess-pink sheets were my shield.

Surely a little bit of critical thinking in those moments could have led to the realization that this large, scary monster didn't exist, and if he did, he couldn't possibly fit under my tiny bed. But fear overrode reasoning, and in my captivity, I'd lie motionless and speechless under my sheets. Every shaky breath I took was coordinated so I didn't alert this enemy lurking under my bed. This "threat" held me captive without ever presenting a real threat.

As we grow up, the monsters do too, but now they operate under new names and in new territories. Today we call them anxiety, depression, and loneliness, and we battle them in our heads rather than under our beds. Those lurking monsters hide in our day-to-day activities, often still evoking a fear louder than our faith or reasoning.

Anxiety monsters, as I like to call them, lurk in the corners of our reasoning. Like the make-believe beasts under our beds, they scare us into a motionless and speechless position. These seem more intimidating than our childhood fears because they're connected to not-so-make-believe situations, such as losing someone we love, loving someone who doesn't return the feeling, or feeling a symptom that could lead to a terminal diagnosis. These are apprehensions that twist our reality with a worrisome what-if. Giving in to such thoughts creates a dreary rain cloud over our future and steals the sunshine from our present. What's one to do when caught in the downpour? For all we know, we could overcome them the same way we could have defeated the green monster of our youth—with rhyme and reason.

For years, anxiety crept into every room I entered and kept me trapped in isolation. But one day I awakened to the truth. I had allowed anxiety to strip me of my peace, confidence, and voice. I became infuriated enough to fight back. The Bible says the enemy comes to steal, kill, and destroy. Friend, it's the truth. Such words can seem exaggerated, but I cannot overemphasize how true they are, especially when it comes to our mental health. If your peace has been stolen, your joy killed, and your hope destroyed, you've encountered an enemy-sent anxiety monster.

Have you been there? Are you ready to fight and expose the anxiety monsters that have robbed you? Then let's do this—together. They say that curiosity killed the cat, but when it comes to anxiety, our lack thereof can be the real detriment. Maybe asking the right questions can help us find the right path to healing. Our fears and anxieties are often written off as common modern-day ailments, but what if they're actually side effects? Have you ever asked yourself the following?

"When did my anxious thinking begin?"
"Where could it be stemming from?"
"How can I put a stop to it?"

You don't have to suffer with this way of thinking. You can cultivate strength and peace that allow you to be whole again! Anxiety is tough to discuss because there are various levels and types, and they cause people to respond differently. Of course, I do not aim to diagnose the level you've experienced, but I do want to offer biblical and practical help I've used and researched to disclose the enemy's tactics. Ultimately, I believe there are a few steps we can take to alleviate anxious thinking. In this chapter we will face off with the three questions above and discover plausible answers and treatments so we can expose and disarm that which steals our peace and present!

Unmask Your Fears

I'll be the first to admit I can be a scaredy cat at times—tall heights, great white sharks, outer space—these are some of the more terrifying fears in my life. This is how I know for a fact that God didn't call me to be an astronaut. (Sorry to let you down, NASA.) I pass on horror films or at least cover my eyes for half the movie if someone manages to twist my arm enough to watch one. But strangely enough, I've always enjoyed mysteries. Perhaps it's the problem-solving, the sorting through clues, or the fact that life itself is a mystery of sorts, but whatever it is, I'm a sucker for a good detective-required puzzle.

Before you were old enough to watch those gory horror films, you may have gotten your thriller fix on Saturday mornings with Scooby-Doo and the Mystery Gang as they solved baffling crimes while facing off with the strangest and scariest foes. The Mystery Gang would outwit ghosts, robots, mummies, or some type of monster in every episode. We don't have to dig too far in our memory banks to recall images of Shaggy and Scooby shivering together in teeth-chattering fear as they yelled, "Zoinks!"

Thinking back on the show now as an adult, what sticks out to me is the inspiring ending of each episode. No matter how terrifying, evil, or sinister the monster appeared, when the gang finally caught the culprit, it was always a mere man or woman hiding behind a mask. They were never as scary as the gang had determined them to be, and it was often someone they knew. Their terror was based on the illusion the monster's mask personified, not who was actually behind the mask.

Our monsters are scariest when they're mysterious.

Once the Scooby-Doo gang could see the monsters for who they truly were, their anxiety was swept away. Is it really that simple? Can we do the same with our anxiety monsters? Perhaps. For those of you who have been riddled with anxious thoughts, overwhelming circumstances, or fearful mindsets, know you're not alone. Sometimes, that simple knowing makes what you're facing less frightening. I won't pretend to have all the answers when it comes to anxiety. In fact, I have few foolproof solutions. But what I do have is a testimony and a knowledge of God's nature. And when we are scared or lost, that's the best thing we can trust in.

For years anxiety monsters crept into every room I entered and kept me trapped in isolation. This was because I imagined everyone saw me as less than, with all my mistakes and insecurities on display. Anytime things fell apart in my life, I fell with them. I'd break down in my bathroom, crying endlessly with the shower running to hide the sound of my sobs. If I made a mistake, I'd disappear into my mind, becoming a zombie to those around me. Unable to overcome what I felt and thought in those moments, I was instantly that little girl hiding under the sheets again. There's a reason many refer to it as "crippling anxiety," because it does just that—it paralyzes you or breaks your stride until you develop a limp.

So how do we overcome anxiety? First, we have to remove the mask. Ironically enough, the Mystery Gang never defeated any monster they came up against. They exposed them. This may seem less courageous or heroic, but it takes just as much bravery and even more brains. If you've ever been paralyzed by anxiety, you might remember how easy it is to believe "there's just no beating this"—and you're right. That form of anxiety, in most cases, has been largely fueled by the power you've given it in your headspace. You can't beat it because part of its hold is you. Yes, *you*. Anxiety is a partnership of real-world problems and predicaments, plus your own worrisome thoughts. It's the seen and the unseen that create the lethal weapon. But what does that weapon look like when you remove the mask? When you take back the power you've given it? By removing the mask of the part you play, you can gain the momentum to fight back.

What we fear is often scarier in our heads than it is in reality. For Scooby and the gang, the three-thousand-year-old mummy was scarier than the treasure-hungry doctor. For us, what we anticipate or dread is often more overwhelming than our real circumstances. The first step to breaking anxiety is to demystify the situation. This action is defined as "to make something easier to understand and less complicated by explaining it in a clear and simple way."[1] Anyone, a timid six-year-old girl or a brilliant professor, can demystify. We don't need to be the bravest or smartest. When we apply rhyme and reason to what we're walking through, we often find our footing.

Say you're a college student who's overwhelmed by what's on your plate and scared you won't make it through a tough class. You start wondering what your life will look like if you don't graduate. You'll have to move back in with your parents, get a minimum-wage job, and struggle to pay your student loans. Do you see how quickly that escalated from one initial worry? Demystifying our anxieties first and foremost allows us to face them in the present instead of battling the future too. We don't want to be the people in scary movies running in a panic without rationally thinking through our next step. Know that even if you're scared right now, you can be afraid *and* rational simultaneously; you just need to focus on your next step.

And which of you by being anxious can add a single hour to his span of life? (Matt. 6:27 ESV)

Worry only further masks your anxieties, making them seem even scarier and giving them more control. I believe that under the mask of worry, you have more answers than you know. And even if you don't have all the answers, processing and moving in the right direction demystifies what you're facing, and slowly the haze fades, allowing you to see each problem and step more clearly. If you were scared you were falling behind in class, what could you do to make it through? You could up your study hours, talk through class points with a friend, or get a tutor. Real problems require real solutions.

Real problems require real solutions.

If you remember the old tale of the hare and the tortoise, the tortoise crosses the finish line first, because unlike the hare, he keeps moving forward—one step at a time. The Bible says God's thoughts are higher than our thoughts and His ways higher than our ways (Isa. 55:8–9). Take heart in the fact that we cannot see how it all works out, but it's not our duty to process and plan it all out. Have you ever walked into the ocean and been suddenly taken out by an unexpected wave as tall as you are? Your feet fly up, saltwater rushes up your nose, and you likely have at least one piece of your swimsuit out of place when you make it back up for air. That's a parallel to anxious thinking.

It attempts to sweep us off our feet, drown us in confusion, and misplace our hope in who we are. The enemy wants us to take it all in at once. He wants us to feel the burden that only God can uphold. Applying rational thinking and problem-solving removes the mask the enemy hides behind. Like the villains at the end of the Scooby-Doo episodes, his tricks are thwarted by removing his mask. "And I would have gotten away with it too, if it weren't for ~~you meddling kids~~ your rational thinking!"

We must look expectantly toward the future instead of worrying about it. Make the five-year plan, write down your goals, pin your dream wedding on Pinterest if you want to, but do it all in hope, not worry. You don't need to pick out your reception colors or know how you're going to afford your unborn kid's college tuition just yet. There is plenty to plan later and enjoy today.

Put on Your Cape

What if you're battling the kind of anxiety that causes you to question not only your college grades but also your entire existence? Deep-set anxiety and depression often lead us to label ourselves as castaways. Washed ashore by the waves and undercurrents, we think we're lucky just to catch a breath of air.

When a passenger falls overboard from a vessel ship, the first thing someone does is throw them a life buoy. It's a helpful tool to keep us afloat, but if I were adrift in the middle of the sea clinging to this doughnut of a flotation device without the ability to swim, I'd still be terrified. Why? Because if I'm an anxious person in an anxious situation, it doesn't matter how many resources I have, I'm still going to think the same way. "What if this piece is flawed? What if I slip out from it or it can't support me? What if the same whale that swallowed Jonah comes for me next?" It doesn't matter what tricks, resources, or comforts we have to tune out anxiety if we don't know how to actually fight back. What if instead of being ruled by the waves and dependent on what or who is around us, we could learn how to swim?

A life buoy will help you stay afloat if you're thrown overboard, but what about the next time? Will there be one then? Can we put all our faith in the hope that the right person will be in the right spot with the right resource at the right time? If you ask the realist in me, the answer is no. I'm thankful for every friend and family member who was a shoulder to cry on or a listening ear when I battled anxiety. I do believe they were a part of my healing process. But the main person who was the deciding factor in my freedom was me. If you've been tossed by the sea of anxiety, the best thing you can learn to do is swim or at least keep your head above the water.

For years I believed my anxious thoughts and behaviors were part of my cracked core—that they were inescapable because they were part of me. But the day I awakened to the truth that *I* had allowed anxiety to strip me of my peace, confidence, and voice, I got mad. Mad enough to change the narrative. I decided I wasn't going to keep being thrown overboard if I could help it—I was going to hold on to something firm.

When we face our fears, we will see that they're less scary, less powerful, and less mysterious than we have worked them up to be. It's time we stand up to what's trying to rob us of living our most beautiful lives. Take that bedsheet you've been hiding under and wrap it around yourself as a cape instead. Corra Mae Harris, one of the first female war correspondents to report from overseas during WWI, is often credited with this advice: "The bravest thing you can do when you are not brave is to profess courage and act accordingly."

Amid a giant storm at sea, the disciples woke Jesus in a frantic plea to (in their opinion) get Him to care that they were dying. According to Mark 4:39, "And he awoke and rebuked the wind and said to the sea, 'Peace! Be still!' And the wind ceased, and there was a great calm" (ESV). When we read this verse, we may think, *Yes, God, take this anxiety away! I, too, was near death, and if you care for me, you will take it all away!* Well . . . that's not what this means.

Have you ever watched a heroic film in which, in a magical moment, the scary dragon or menacing villain just disappears halfway through? Would you even pay money to see that movie? Most likely not! Because while we enjoy a happy ending, we watch stories of heroes who teach and inspire us to be heroic ourselves. Villains aren't written out of the plot, because even in fiction, doing so would feel false to the champion's journey. This reminds me of our trials in life. I know I've personally made the request more than once, "God, please make this problem stop." Yet it doesn't always happen that way.

Sometimes the rain ends after a few sprinkles, other times the tempest rages for what seems like an eternity. The comfort we have in both situations is that God remains in control and by our side.

When Jesus informed us that this earth will present challenges we must walk through (John 16:33), He also assured us He'd never ever, in a million years, leave us to face them alone (Deut. 31:8). He will *always* be with us!

I cannot put myself in your shoes, and I will not pretend the problems we face are not fear-provoking. But I do appeal to you not to consider what you've experienced to be due to God's lack of care for you. Right before He calmed the winds in the story from Mark 4, Jesus's disciples questioned His concern for their lives. "Teacher, do you not care that we are perishing?" (v. 38 ESV). He responded, "Why are you so afraid?" (v. 40 ESV). Our mortal view of good versus bad is primitive in contrast to God's. He sees the bigger picture and saw it long before our worry was in attendance. When your emotions rise and your soul feels seasick, remember His goodness is at work! He's reframing what the enemy intended for evil and developing us all at once. For the Bible tells us so:

> "For I know the plans I have for you," declares the LORD, "plans to prosper you and not to harm you, plans to give you hope and a future. Then you will call on me and come and pray to me, and I will listen to you." (Jer. 29:11–12)

> Consider it pure joy, my brothers and sisters, whenever you face trials of many kinds, because you know that the testing of your faith produces perseverance. Let perseverance finish its work so that you may be mature and complete, not lacking anything. (James 1:2–4)

> And the God of all grace, who called you to his eternal glory in Christ, after you have suffered a little while, will himself restore you and make you strong, firm and steadfast. (1 Pet. 5:10)

God gives you internal strength to face your external problems. Somewhere within, there's a fighter. Let her loose! Part of breaking up with the anxieties that broke you is facing them. We must first win the war in our minds, telling our faith to rise in the battle. God doesn't hand us magic wands to chase away the spooks; He gives us a far better tool—the gospel! The gospel is the good news of the cross. It gives us peace come what may, because we know who holds the final victory.

When this faith hits us like a surge of adrenaline, it's like when our childhood selves kicked the monsters out from under the bed. With the cape of the gospel, we can take what we once hid behind and leverage it to our advantage. The knowledge of His Word allows our faith to permeate even the deepest anxiety within us as we put our hope and trust in the One who is and is yet to come. "For you did not receive the spirit of slavery to fall back into fear, but you have received the Spirit of adoption as sons, by whom we cry, 'Abba! Father!'" (Rom 8:15 ESV).

Use Your Voice

It can be disturbing to list the real-life dangers that lurk in our world. And we don't have to venture far to find them either. We've all heard the fear-provoking stories of women targeted outside a store like Walmart, followed while on a jog alone, or cornered at a big event. It's a frightening reality that things like this happen. What are we women to do? How do we prepare for the worst-case scenarios?

You may think your only defense is to carry a firearm or travel with pepper spray, but you already have the most useful weapon in your arsenal—your voice. In the chance of an attack, your voice is lethal for four reasons:

- It's within quick access.
- It catches the attacker off guard.
- It alerts others to come to your aid.
- It activates your adrenaline.

Think this is all hullabaloo? Read what Strategic Living, a self-defense training company, writes as a cautionary message to their customers: "Those who choose to target women are hoping for a target who can be easily intimidated into silence. They are not looking for a feisty contest."[2]

If you yell "fire" in a packed theater or "shark" in an ocean full of swimmers, you'll have everyone on the move in seconds. A single word will initiate motion. What you speak both aloud and to yourself influences the world around you. Notice the way you talk about your current anxieties. Perhaps you say things like,

- "I'm just an anxious person."
- "I can't do it. I'm not capable."
- "That's way too scary."

What do these words say to your brain? When you speak in this manner, you evoke an attitude of defeat before you even enter the fight. Such words signal an unsound loss. Using your voice in a negative tone is as detrimental as not using it at all. Just as you would in a real attack, use your voice to fight your fears.

Your voice is precise, and your words are powerful.

Anne Frank spoke through pen and paper. Billie Holiday sang for change. Helen Keller signed to speak on behalf of others. How you use your voice may differ from the woman beside you, but the world needs what you bring to the table. You may not be the loudest in the room, but that doesn't mean your message isn't loud. Your authority is not dependent on pitch, perception, or perfection. If your hands shake or your voice trembles, you're still on the right path.

Remember, if all instruments sounded the same, there would be no symphonies. You don't have to speak or sound the same as someone else for your voice to carry weight. Discover the notes and chords you were designed to perform.

Kind words are like honey—
  sweet to the soul and healthy for the body. (Prov. 16:24
  NLT)

Start speaking encouragement over yourself and over your future and see how fear melts at the sound. You'll catch the devil off guard when you speak words true to the Word and contrary to his attacks.

Fear the Lord

What do Adele, Barbra Streisand, and Rihanna all have in common? Well, besides them all having phenomenal vocal cords, each woman has admitted to battling stage fright, or performance anxiety, before concerts.[3] *Celebrities, they're just like us!* Even powerhouse singers aren't exempt from feeling butterflies or worrying about a performance simply because they're professionals. Instead, they have to face their fears each time they take the stage and ask which is stronger: their passion to perform or their fear of the crowd.

Franklin D. Roosevelt said, "Courage is not the absence of fear, but rather the assessment that something else is more important than fear."[4] Do not confuse being courageous for being fearless. Your favorite heroines, leaders, and even performers don't have a superhuman trait for eliminating fear. They have courage. Courage is how we make it through trying times, difficult circumstances, and scary possibilities. It's often rooted in a deep belief or tied to something bigger than us.

Let's talk about a woman in the Bible who had good reason to be anxious—Abigail. She's noted as the intelligent and beautiful wife of Nabal, a wealthy man with lots of livestock in the desert David escaped to when he had to flee Saul. To make a long story short, David checked on this guy's cattle while he was there, and whenever he and his men were low on resources, he sent a messenger to say, "Hey, man, we're getting kinda hungry over here.

Could you return the favor and send some food? 'Preciate ya!" Nabal had an abundance of rations to offer, but he also had an abundance of attitude. He gave David's messengers a message of his own: "Nah, I'm good."

As you'd imagine, David wasn't particularly pleased with that. So, what'd he do? The surely tired and hangry future king told four hundred of his men, "Strap on your sword!" (1 Sam. 25:13). Aka "This means war!" He and his men set off to return the favor that Nabal had so generously gifted them. One of Nabal's servants warned Abigail of the impending danger and how no one in the entire home could talk sense into Nabal, leaving the ball in her court as to how to respond. She could have made one of three moves:

A) Do nothing and await the effects of her husband's surly actions.

B) Grab what she could for herself and take off for the hills.

C) Attempt to make amends.

If four hundred men with swords were charging to my home in the heat of vengeance, you had best believe I'd be shaking in my boots. But Abigail chose courage over fear. She didn't let the impending threat keep her stagnant, and she didn't run away to save only herself. She quickly gathered food, wine, and cattle to take to David and his men, hoping she could assuage his anger and halt the attack.

In that period, anyone who approached a strong leader in such a way, especially a woman, was gambling their life. Not only was Abigail brave, but she was also honorable. The story says when she saw him, she fell at David's feet asking for forgiveness for her husband's folly. Moved by her words and bravery, David accepted her request and blessed her in return.

Her why was greater than her fear. Her courage saved not only her life but also the lives of those in her household. She stepped up where she saw lack. No excuses, no holding back, no resentment—

only a brave woman with offerings in her hands and blessings on her tongue. The best part is, she didn't have to do it either. That's why her story is so impactful. We can break up with anxiety in our own life to find personal freedom, but channeling courage can issue freedom for us *and* others. Who else could benefit from your triumphs? What domino effect might occur from your bravery?

When we live for more than our own interest and gain, we tap into more courage than we have on our own. There is something greater than your anxiety, something more important than your fears. What's important is not if you fall or fail in the future but that you keep moving forward. Ahead lies an assignment with your name on it, if you persevere.

When Abigail's husband fell at the hand of the Lord a few days later (note to self: don't be like Nabal!), David asked for Abigail's hand in marriage. Based on how she reacted to the anxiety-invoking moment earlier, she could have been slaughtered or long gone on the run, but instead, she became the wife of the coming ruler of Israel. Rarely can we foresee what our bravery will lead to, but in the end, we'll be thankful we responded with courage.

We will face real fears in this life, sometimes even due to choosing to do the right thing, like Abigail. But when we act in line with God's will, we know that we are never alone. He goes before us and guides us through any circumstance.

If God is for us, who can be against us? (Rom. 8:31 ESV)

If we are to fear, then let us fear the Lord. This fear may sound contradictory to the courage message, but it is not the same fear we've known. It's a holy reverence for the One who is over all—a rearranging of our priorities, if you will. It doesn't cripple, it empowers. It doesn't dismantle, it upholds. To fear the Lord is to have courage to do His will, even in the face of danger. As the Bible says, it is the beginning of wisdom. This fear is an acknowledgement of His sovereignty and value in our lives. I love the way my father-in-love, John, describes it: "Holy fear is not to be scared of

God and thereby withdraw from Him. It is to be terrified of being away from Him."[5]

I cannot promise that you won't weather storms or venture through rough waves, but I can assure you that as you put your fear in the Lord, He will expand your capacity for courage. He will be the anchor that keeps you steady even as the waves rise and the wind roars (Heb. 6:19). For many of us, what we can control has been our life raft and what we can foresee our compass. I'm asking you to change your operating system. To break up with anxiety is no small feat. Some days may take more courage than others. Keep showing up, especially on those days.

To break up with anxiety, you need to:

1. Unmask your fears.
2. Put on your cape.
3. Use your voice.
4. Fear the Lord.

Anxiety monsters try to steal our future through intimidation. But as we rise to face what frightens us, we will see those monsters aren't as scary as we are strong. God gave you a voice to speak with authority, and as much as he tries, the enemy will never be able to take that away from you. If you fight anxiety with rational thinking, courage, and your voice, you will be victorious. Make the enemy regret ever thinking you were an easy target. With God by our side, whom and what shall we fear?!

04. Breaking Comparisons

A flower does not think of competing to the flower next to it.
It just blooms.

—Sensei Ogui

They just don't make them like they used to!

As I've purchased toys and games for my son, I've noticed how different our playtimes—or should I really say screen times—were compared to those of kids today. Fortunately, there are some great items for children today that don't require AA batteries, and I'm thankful I grew up with solid options for fueling hands-on imagination and creativity. How many of you are old enough to remember Lite-Brites, Easy-Bake Ovens, or Mr. Potato Head? Classics! One of my personal favorite toys was none other than Barbie. There was something magical about playing make-believe. You could give your doll the dream life—a closet full of pretty pink clothes, elite status in her Barbie Dreamhouse, and hunky Ken wrapped around her finger. Yep, life in plastic sure was fantastic!

Barbie was the first "supermodel" many of us knew—perfect, pristine, and untouchable. She was a shining example of what we wanted—and expected—to be when we grew up. But as we got older, we focused on our own escapades. It became time to create our own dream life—find the right career, loyal friends, and the dream guy . . . *if* they were all out there to be found. But as we grew, instead of simply putting our Barbie away on a shelf, many of us put her on a pedestal.

That dream life we gave her was the one we thought *we* needed. But when we sought to fulfill those desires, we found things didn't come as easy in the real world as they did in our imagination. We began to ask why. Why couldn't we land the job, find the friends, or meet the guy? It must have been because unlike polished, plastic Barbie, we had our fair share of imperfections. And just like that, comparison snuck in. We started to believe the lie that in order for our own life to have significance, it had to look like someone else's.

This mindset hit me hard when I was a teenager. I had long since stopped playing with my childhood toys, but the Barbie effect lingered. I started admiring the girls who I saw as real-life Barbies—seemingly perfect blond bombshells whose lives were wrapped with a bow. I thought they had something I didn't, something I never would. Be it their stunning looks, airy dispositions, or polished lives, these girls were the ideal standard of what I was *supposed* to be. You know the girls I'm talking about—the prom queen, your high school crush's crush, the head cheerleader dating the quarterback. The girls you studied to see what kind of clothes they were wearing and the "cool" way they talked.

Why can't I be like them?

Their untainted beauty and polished perfection were enough to make me tuck my head in inferiority, like a dog admitting defeat. I wasn't in an actual competition with these girls, but I didn't need to be. In my mind, I'd already come in last place. I separated myself as a subclass under these seemingly perfect women and was ashamed I couldn't measure up to their standards.

Have you ever diminished yourself or believed you were less than someone else? Fixating on what another person has to offer will always make you question what you bring to the table. It's hard enough just trying to discover who you are, but when you add the pressures of high school insecurity, college competition, or workplace vying, it just gets messier.

If you paused right now and took three minutes to draw a flower, I bet it'd look rather lovely. But if you took an additional five minutes to stare at the drawing, you'd slowly begin to think less and less of it. If you took another five minutes to review others' drawings, you'd travel deeper down that thought pattern. Why do we do this? Why do we fixate on our mistakes yet prize others' successes? Must everything be a competition?

Comparison is a lurking, nagging thought that lives in our heads rent free. It envelops our initiatives and actions in a shroud of smoke and mirrors, twisting the good nature of who we are and what we do. We put others' looks, accomplishments, and dispositions on a pedestal, but our own on a shelf. Comparison looks down on us and permeates our minds until it affects our outlook, confidence, and hope.

Comparison is cancerous.

Those feelings of inadequacy and insecurity spread from one area to the next. I started talking down to myself in a way that seems almost unfathomable now. "You're just not as pretty as she is, not as talented as they are. Why would you even try? You're not half as good as so and so." I adopted the idea that others were truly better than me, point-blank. At this level, I subconsciously pitted myself against others again and again and placed my worth and abilities lower and lower. At the height of my comparison, it didn't matter if anyone else thought I was talented, beautiful, or deserving, because I stopped believing I was.

Maybe it's not so hard to imagine that because you've been there yourself. You left the fight because someone "better" was in the ring. But here's the truth: comparison is a broken practice. It does not produce accurate or beneficial results. It's broken by design, and it attempts to break those caught in its trap. This is why you must break up with this way of thinking. You have potential. You have purpose. But comparison will contort and dismiss both. If you want to discover that special life worth living, you need to understand what comparison is and does—and break up with it.

Girl, Don't Dare Compare

I'd like to say that when I graduated high school, I graduated from this mentality of thinking less of myself too, but that's not true. I had allowed it to take root so deeply and for so long that it became synonymous with my identity—yet it wasn't feeding me the way a healthy root system does. It was feeding off my shame and insecurity, affecting how I looked, what I said, and even how I showed up in life.

I feel God detailed this truth for me in a dream one night.

Walking around the Louvre Museum, I found myself alone. Suddenly a guide approached me, saying, "Congratulations! You are taking one of these exquisite pieces of art home today, but be careful, because you can only pick one." I began my search and quickly found the *Mona Lisa*. Instantly, I knew it was the one; that was my painting! The guide reappeared and asked if I was pleased with my choice.

"Yes, without a shadow of a doubt this is my painting."

"Beautiful choice," he replied, "but before you go, why don't you take another look at the other paintings just to be sure?" To oblige his request, I continued my study of the gallery. Why not? It was one of the most exquisite art exhibitions, after all. The farther I ventured, the more doubt crept over me.

If you know anything about the *Mona Lisa*, you know it's an abnormal attraction. The colors are muted, and the figure holds a questionable grin.

As I examined the other pieces around the gallery, I noticed that unlike mine, some had gold embellishments and vibrant color. *Is my piece of art lacking something important? Is this the right choice?* I thought. The guide joined me once more and echoed, "Are you still happy with your painting?"

"No," I replied. "My painting doesn't have what these others do."

With a look of understanding but a sobering tone, the guide cautioned, "If you give up your painting, you're giving up the most famous painting in the world."

We cannot elevate or denote our significance or beauty by contrasting ourselves to God's other works of art. Comparison strips us of joy because it shifts our eyes from Creator to creation. But we were never designed to idolize anything aside from Him.

See, comparison doesn't come only for our accomplishments; its bigger target is our worth. We start by thinking someone else's art is more pleasing or their look is prettier than ours. Then we begin thinking their purpose is grander, life is better, or value is greater. What's happening? Each time we dig at an area of our life, we taint its beauty. When we live in a comparing mindset for long enough, it corrupts the very core of how we see ourselves. When we get dressed in the morning, we won't see ourselves in the mirror; we'll see the woman we "should" look like. When we go for the job interview, we won't speak from the heart; we'll give the rehearsed narrative of what we "should" say.

I remember being a freshman in college and eating only once or twice a day to lose enough weight by spring break so I could stomach standing next to all the beach-babe beauties. After weeks of cutting carbs and counting calories, I arrived a few pounds lighter but carried even more emotional weight than before. All the dieting, sulking, and self-loathing wasn't doing me any good. I still felt the same—insecure and unimpressive. And I knew why.

I wasn't ever going to look like someone else, because the only person's image I was meant to strive after was Christ's.

I wasn't ever going to look like someone else, because the only person's image I was meant to strive after was Christ's.

Too many of us have suffered from eating disorders, mental health issues, and identity stigmas as dangerous by-products of comparison. If you've been there, please hear my heart as these words are intended to unveil your true beauty. Comparison tricks us into believing others are better than we are and that we somehow don't measure up. But God doesn't desire us to be anyone else. He's much more invested in our original design.

I awoke from that dream and swiftly reached for my phone to see if the museum guide's statement was true. Sure enough, a quick Google search proved the *Mona Lisa* is the most famous and heavily insured painting in the world.

In waking from that dream, I awoke to a new understanding of just how intricate God's love is for each and every one of His daughters. Every piece of art is unique—the only one of its kind and unlike anything else. So are you. You are His masterpiece. His prize. His unique expression.

Know the True Thief

Comparison isn't always measuring apples to oranges; sometimes it's counting someone's basketful of apples while yours sits empty. Whenever you're in a season of waiting or wondering, it can be tempting to contrast your timeline to someone else's. But there's a truth you and I must hold to in these times—and certainly not because it's easy, but because it's essential to what God is doing: someone else's blessings aren't robbing you of yours.

I used to think blessings were like lunar eclipses—transient. Once one passes, you have to wait the full lunar phase to see one again. But God doesn't operate through our perception of time. He's not confined to a pattern or a single way of execution. His plan is unlike anything we are used to or can predict.

Our Creator isn't small-minded either. What God has for us isn't taken when someone else experiences something similar. And it won't come sooner when others are desiring the same thing. Maybe one way to break up with comparison is to stop looking up at the moon and wishing on stars to get what we want and instead start bowing our heads in prayer.

Jesus performed countless miracles throughout His ministry on this earth, so many that it's believed the stories recorded in the New Testament are only a fraction of what His followers saw (John 20:30). But in the miracles we are privy to read about thousands of years later, I believe there are details and lessons ripe for the picking that could become breakthrough moments in our lives today.

Someone else's blessings aren't robbing you of yours.

For example, John 5 shares an account of a man considered an invalid who spent his days near the pools of Bethesda. Now, these weren't the same as modern-day luxury pools; these were medicinal ponds at best. Bethesda, like many other ancient cities, had these community areas designated to serve as public bathhouses and hopeful miracle grounds. If someone was determined to be "unclean," they would use these public baths essentially for ritual purification and cleansing. Those who were blind, lame, and paralyzed bathed there. These pools, or *mikvehs*, were a sort of washing for the lower class devoid of the joy and freedom that comes with a true baptism.[1]

Until Jesus.

Verse 5 tells us that the man had been crippled for thirty-eight years and spent his days lying by the pools waiting for a miracle. When Jesus came to the city and encountered the man, he asked an audacious question: "Do you want to be healed?" (v. 6 ESV). The first time I read this passage, I thought surely Jesus was having a cocky moment, like a jock asking if you want to see how far he can throw a football. Or that He had been so immersed in a conversation with Peter and John that He hadn't noted how obviously this man was in need of a miracle. But like every other action Jesus performed, and every other word breathed in Scripture, this was intentional. Jesus knew the man's situation, and He knew his heart.

The invalid answered, "Sir, I have no one to put me into the pool when the water is stirred up, and while I am going another steps down before me" (v. 7 ESV). I want to point out that when Jesus asked him if he wanted his nearly four-decades-long problem alleviated, he answered with the issues and people preventing it. But here's the thing—what God wants to do in our lives is not dependent on or limited by what we consider limitations. If God has your name on it, there's no mistake. Don't confuse others as competition when they're actually community. Our callings, purposes, and passions are amplified through service and relationships.

I have full empathy for this man, who must have been saddened by years of pain and struggle. Jesus told the man, "Get up, take up your bed, and walk" (v. 8 ESV). In one moment, the man's ailment was fully alleviated. At once his body was healed, and in a manner different than he'd been expecting! Turns out no one was in the way of his miracle at all. He never even got in the water! Rather, his healing came from another person, and his heart was what got baptized (v. 14).

Why did Jesus add "take up your bed"? This man wasn't resting on a valuable, queen-size, memory foam mattress. This bed would have been a small, dirty, rolled-up mat just big enough for him to lie on. It was a symbol that God's workings can't be confined to religious opinion or altered by human views. He knows what He's doing, plus when and why He's doing it.

What would the mat represent for you if you were the person in this encounter? Have you been lying on a tainted self-view, staring at how everything is working out for everyone else? Have you made your bed with the idea that you just got the short end of the stick? Take up your bed and walk. I'm unable to tell you the whats, whens, or whys in your life, but I can tell you the who—Jesus. He is intentional with every season and second of your life! The only thing we need to know is who He is; the rest rests in His healing hands.

Identify where comparison has broken your thoughts, passion, or hope so you can move forward in the direction of faith! I don't have to tell you how easy it is to look at all the good that is happening for others and think you're missing out. Perhaps you've been praying for your dream job for months, going to interview after interview without any luck, only to have your best friend get hers after randomly meeting someone in a coffee shop. Or perhaps you've been praying to conceive a child for years and thought you might be pregnant, but when you took a test, the screen read negative—right before a friend's baby shower.

These are real problems. But, my friend, in your resolve and in your courage to keep believing, I pray discouragement doesn't give rise to doubt. Do scenarios such as these mean we are less than? That God's blessings will never rest on us if we experience doubt? Certainly not! The Word assures us that God hears our prayers and provides every blessing.

> So, my very dear friends, don't get thrown off course. Every desirable and beneficial gift comes out of heaven. The gifts are rivers of light cascading down from the Father of Light. There is nothing deceitful in God, nothing two-faced, nothing fickle. He brought us to life using the true Word, showing us off as the crown of all his creatures. (James 1:16–18 MSG)

> And this is the confidence that we have toward him, that if we ask anything according to his will he hears us. And if we know that he hears us in whatever we ask, we know that we have the requests that we have asked of him. (1 John 5:14–15 ESV)

This is as good a time as any to pause and clarify what is meant by "God's blessings." God wants His people to prosper. Not in a "prosperity gospel" or "genie in a bottle" kind of way, but in a manner of care. He doesn't want you happy and rich or hungry and reduced; He wants you to live holy and righteous.

Some of the most influential individuals throughout the Bible were blessed in very different ways. For example, King Solomon was wealthy and had many wives, while Paul's income was based on scattered donations and he is thought to have been single by choice or widowed. But both men were chosen, cared for, and blessed by God.

Everything we have is gifted to us from the Father. This leads us to see that it's not prescribed or profitable to compare blessings. For Paul himself, who'd be seen as the "lesser" or "lacking" if compared to Solomon, writes,

> Not that we dare to classify or compare ourselves with some of those who are commending themselves. But when they measure themselves by one another and compare themselves with one another, they are without understanding. (2 Cor. 10:12 ESV)

The good thing God is doing in someone else's life doesn't hijack what He's doing in yours. The real opponent to believing and receiving God's gifts is the one who wants to thwart or steal them. Because we have a God who's written us a beautiful future, we have an enemy who wants to destroy it. But he's no match for God, so he will try to weave comparison into your life. He can't steal your blessings, so he'll try to steal your joy, fruitfulness, and intimacy with God. Of course, he'd love nothing more than for you to not realize your value and overlook your importance. And I can't help but think how much this hurts the Father's heart even more than our own.

The grass will seem greener on someone else's lawn if you're not watering yours well. We experienced this the other day when my husband pointed out how lush our neighbor's yard was compared to ours, which was brittle and brown. I thought back to how much their sprinklers would run both in the morning and evening, so I asked him, "Well, are we prepared to water our grass as much as they do?"

Are you prepared to make some changes? Are you ready to give God back your hope and faith? Are you ready to shift your focus from the outcomes and timelines to your efforts and mindset? I believe there's so much good ahead of you, so much green grass that these efforts will not be in vain.

Don't Let Go(gh) of Your Joy

There is truly no one like you. That's more than a cute, comforting line. Within your physical being you have a specific DNA code. Unlike a building blueprint that can be copied, your human genome cannot. Even identical twins experience cell growth and mutations in the womb that create unique expressions and differentiating features and characteristics. Isn't that fascinating? If siblings from the same sperm and egg can still have their own unique features, there's hardly any scientific ground to say, "Well, I don't bring anything special to the table." Hogwash! Rubbish! Preposterous! Any way you say it, that's nonsense.

If you're still thinking, *Okay, sure, I'm different, but different isn't always good, Christian*, then let's go there! We've already mentioned the legendary piece by Leonardo da Vinci called the *Mona Lisa*, but let's talk about another well-known artist, one who also felt different—Vincent van Gogh. Did you know that during his lifetime he was considered a lost cause along with his art? As a boy, he was shy and had low self-esteem, and shockingly, he sold only one painting in his lifetime.[2] Today, however, van Gogh is known as one of the greatest Postimpressionist artists of all time, and his unique pieces sell for millions of dollars. So maybe different isn't so bad, after all. Maybe the feeling of being different is a by-product of our unique DNA.

I want to challenge you not to see yourself as any of the broken identities we've tackled. You are not anxious, insecure, robbed, less than, left out, or too different. When we break up with who we're not, we create space to discover who our incomparable God created us to be.

There is a joy that comes from discovering who we are and why we're here. This is partially because it's a spiritual phenomenon and partially, I've concluded, because it removes the flesh's need for comparison. With a firm image to look to, our once-frantic questioning of "Who am I?" calms to a steady gaze set on Jesus, and from it, we get a clear view of ourselves. As Hebrews 12:1–2 says, "And let us run with perseverance the race marked out for us, fixing our eyes on Jesus, the pioneer and perfecter of faith."

Breaking up with comparison may feel like ripping off a bandage only to find the wound underneath isn't so pretty. But, sis, it's healing. That's what restoring a cut looks like. Before we can have an exterior that's pretty again, we have to cleanse what's within. All the self-help books may not tell you this, but the only way to feel confident in your skin is to set your identity in Christ, fixing your eyes on Him.

Remember, Plastic Isn't Always Fantastic

Earlier we talked about how comparing our accomplishments and looks to others can taint our self-worth. The same is true for comparing our pasts. One thing I've recognized about the self-deprecating webs we weave is that they start from one strand. When our pasts look "worse" than others, we slip into shame. When we're stuck in shame, we begin to regret. See that web growing larger? That's why this section of uncovering is crucial!

Even after I addressed my habit of comparing myself to others in regard to my looks and accomplishments, I had to relearn how not to compare my past to others too. When I began dating Arden, he made me feel set apart and special, like I was the only girl in the world. And the day he got down on one knee, I realized he was promising to love me for life . . . *me*! I wasn't one of those prim and perfect girls with squeaky-clean backgrounds his parents had probably introduced to him in church; I came with baggage, skeletons in my closet, and a list of shortcomings. That devaluing mindset began to conflict with my reality and tried to steal my future.

During our engagement, I remember constantly coming up against the thought that as soon as he realized how flawed I was, he'd throw in the towel. Understand that I knew the things I worried about were in the past, but my past still haunted me like a bad credit score. I thought he'd see that I seemed right for him, but with a broken track record, I couldn't be trusted—or even worse, I was damaged goods. This inner monologue played on for weeks until I concluded that a man as amazing as my fiancé deserved his own Barbie—a beautiful girl who was the perfect, pure, ideal Christian wife. I told God of my discovery and informed Him that He had made some kind of cruel mistake thinking I could marry this wonderful man.

The truth is, a perfect woman without flaws or mistakes comes only in plastic.

Let's pause here and take in the irony of me telling God *my* revelation—like there's any way He'd ever overlook a detail or make a mistake. I think it's a good rule of thumb that if you find yourself informing or correcting God, you don't know what you think you know. But what did He do? Ever so gently, God humored me and said, "Okay, you're right. Can you show me this girl you deem so worthy?"

I couldn't. Because the truth is, a perfect woman without flaws or mistakes comes only in plastic. Even after God brought me out of sin, shame entrapped me to the point that I almost convinced myself I couldn't receive the blessings He was giving me. If you've found yourself in a similar place, ask this: Is shame more powerful than grace?

From Broken to Building Back Better

Many think winning at the game of life is being *the* best, while in reality, we win by being *our* best. The Bible says we are the clay, and He is the potter (Isa. 64:8). God took the time to mold you uniquely. He didn't have anyone else in mind when He made you.

You can walk in godly confidence that every part of who you are was developed with intention and care.

When you break up with comparison, what used to break you can now awaken you. Let it be your shot of espresso. Maybe through this chapter you've realized you've been taking the easy street when it comes to putting in the work of building your dreams, or you've been complaining about what you don't have instead of contending for what you could have, or just maybe you've been blaming God instead of trusting Him. Let's leave those patterns behind and focus on that redeemed, rescued foundation in God. Now's the time to build back better!

Say it with me: "Comparison, we're breaking up!"

No more broken hope.

No more broken dreams.

No more broken confidence.

It's time for change.

We can change our former combative thinking to understand that when someone else is blessed, it's validation that God still moves! Someone else's wins are a cause for celebration, a win for us all. Let it be an amplification to our souls, a refreshing for our faith. Look doubt in the face and say, "Yes, God still does that!" Not only will this keep our hearts from hardening, but it will also fuel our faith for what's coming.

There are still great men to marry.

There are still wild dreams to chase.

There are still victories to be won.

There are still positive pregnancy tests to be celebrated.

There are still chances for success.

There are still breakthroughs to be had.

Comparison fails to show that *what* God gives is just as intentional as *when* He gives it. When we break up with comparison, we can look forward to a new adventure where we have the freedom to discover our own uniqueness—the incomparable, unparalleled qualities God has placed deep within us.

To break up with comparison, you need to:

1. Know the true thief.
2. Don't let go of your joy.
3. Remember, plastic isn't always fantastic.
4. Build back better.

Comparison is unoriginal; self-expression is not. Even if it's messy, the road less traveled is the one worth following. Express yourself with passion, authenticity, honesty, and discipline. Take the call God has placed within you seriously, but don't take yourself too seriously. Allow yourself to make mistakes, but never stop pushing forward.

05. The Shame Game

> Shame loves secrecy. The most dangerous thing to do after a shaming experience is hide or bury our story. When we bury our story, the shame metastasizes.
>
> —Brené Brown

One of the first nods to growing closer to my mother-in-love, Lisa, was when she began passing down her gently loved items to me. If you're like me, this kind of exchange is uniquely bonding.

Last summer, my husband and his father went on a trip while Lisa and I spent the weekend together. Our girl time included everything you'd imagine for perfect mother- and daughter-in-law bonding: an abundance of coffee, delicious ice cream, deep talks, and sharing clothes. Though I'm the spitting image of both my parents combined, when Lisa and I are together, some people assume I'm her biological daughter because of our similar traits and height. This is particularly handy when she passes down those loved items, because we share the same sizes and look good in complementary color tones.

That weekend she gave me an olive-green jumpsuit that she "no longer fit in." (Lisa, I love you, but you're crazy. You're the hottest, fittest g-mama I know.) Later we went to an evening service at church, and I thought, *What a perfect time to wear this while we're together!* I threw on the jumpsuit, cheering that I didn't have to peruse my closet wondering what outfit to wear. But as we reached the church parking lot, I felt something terribly cold on my inner thigh. I turned on the car light to examine, and the realization hit me—there was a gaping hole on the inner seam of one of the pant legs.

Welp! There was no turning back now. We were there and the service was starting. Lisa assured me the hole was not "that big" and no one would notice. But when you have a wardrobe malfunction, you're not rationally thinking how likely it is others will see. You're thinking *everyone* will see it.

Walking into the church, I tried to console myself. As we turned the corner to enter the building, a volunteer photographer jumped out, eagerly snapping in our direction. I dropped my head, trying desperately not to be seen by the camera. Now, to ease your mind, the rip really wasn't that noticeable and showed nothing more than a portion of my winter-pale thigh, but to me, any hole, any skin, any insecurity was too much to bare. (Please laugh at my bad pun to help save my attempt at comedic relief . . . ha ha.)

I sat with Lisa toward the front of the auditorium and tried to put mind over matter. When we stood for worship, I sang along and lifted my hands but kept my feet anchored and my thighs hugged together tightly to hide the rip. Ironically, singing and raising your hands in surrender are some of the most liberating expressions of worship. You release your present worries and stresses of the day to focus freely on God. When you worship, you sing and move, swaying with the rhythm. But at that moment, I was too fixated on keeping my feet firmly planted. As much as I tried to enjoy the incredible worship, I didn't let myself become fully immersed because I thought if I wasn't overly careful, everyone would see.

That's a lot like how we feel about our shame, isn't it? It's a gaping hole we think the entire world can see. Our mistakes, shortcomings, and past all eat away at our peace, identity, and confidence, leaving us hunkered down and hung up on what we can't change. But in reality, we are the only ones who see these areas; what we perceive to be evident is often internal. We keep ourselves stuck by living cautiously instead of freely. We must wake up to the truth that what we think is obvious and detrimental is usually not as bad as we think it is, just like my mother-in-law said. Not a single person made a remark about the hole in my jumpsuit that night. Likewise, no one is discrediting you, and Jesus isn't taken aback by what you're navigating through.

Shame isn't a result of a mistake; it's a by-product of not properly dealing with a mistake.

I got home and realized I had missed out on enjoying where I was because I was worried and ashamed. How much more could I have gotten from the service if I'd believed what Lisa said from the beginning? I don't want you to walk through life and look back with that same disappointment. I want you to break up with any shame you're facing or have carried so that you get the most out of each day and experience. As you identify areas of brokenness and tackle regret, comparison, and anxiety, I want to make sure you continue with the right mindset. It will determine whether you step forward with your head held high or dragging your feet.

Shame isn't a result of a mistake; it's a by-product of not properly dealing with a mistake.

This journey of uncovering what broke you is necessary for your breakthrough. It will allow you to localize what has caused or is causing shame and what it's leading to. Shame is usually the straw that breaks the camel's back when it comes to brokenness. It's a nasty tactic the devil employs as a last attempt to stop someone on the trajectory of moving forward. You've tossed regret, comparison, and anxiety to the side, but shame will continue to hold fast, becoming an emotional ankle weight trying to keep you stagnant or at least slow you down.

Once we know what's gone awry in our lives, we must choose how to move on from it. Knowledge is a tool, after all. But for many of us, shame taints our knowing—of who we are and what we're capable of. To secure the forthcoming promises God has written for us specifically, we must consciously rewire our brains to be shame-free. What does it look like to be free from shame? It's being aware of and apologetic about the broken behaviors of the past without carrying unnecessary weight from them into the future.

My first flight was at seventeen. My mom booked us a flight to Los Angeles for my high school graduation present in the ultimate *Gilmore Girls*–style mother-daughter getaway. As I got ready for the trip, I laid out all my favorite outfits, creating a Pinterest-perfect wardrobe for photo ops and just in case I ran into any celebrities, of course. Better safe than sorry, right? Well, if you've ever flown with anything more than a carry-on, you know that theory does not apply to air travel. Every suitcase and article of clothing adds up—both in your arms and your wallet. I found out the hard way that there's a weight limit to what you carry, and if you exceed it, you'll be paying a fee for what you likely could have left behind. Trust the older, more experienced me—you want to travel efficiently, not excessively. Ditch the baggage of shame before you take off for your future.

Carrying around extra weight only bogs you down. I lugged around tons of outfits I never wore on that trip. They were dead weight. Shame is the same for our mental health and well-being. It doesn't serve us at all; it's only an anchor to where we've been. Our future is bright and meaningful; we should pack accordingly.

If the person we're dating has relationship baggage—they still "hang out" with their ex, they're a habitual cheater, or they have irrational trust issues—a breakup might be necessary, because baggage like this puts a strain on even the healthiest relationships. So it's only fitting that we break up with our emotional baggage. In this chapter, I want to offer four steps that will allow you to live unashamed and lead to your breakthrough.

Listen Closely

There was a viral sensation in 2018 that boggled the minds of many social media users. It was an audio track that seemed to produce two different sounds. It was a conundrum to many, much like the viral blue and black versus white and gold dress debate that preceded it. Yes, these are the mind-stumping issues we dispute in the twenty-first century. The audio appeared to say either *laurel* or *yanny*. In a close tie, 53 percent of people heard *laurel*, while 47 percent of people heard *yanny*.[1] Personally, I heard *laurel* and can't see how people could hear *yanny* while listening to the same sound. But there is a two-part scientific answer to the mystery.

One part of determining which word listeners heard was priming—seeing something beforehand that later influenced perception. Whichever word a listener read first or at the time of the clip playing was likely the one they heard. The other part was dependent on the pitch frequency at which the audio was played or heard. The higher frequency produced the *yanny* sound, while the lower frequency produced the *laurel* sound. While these two words sound vastly different to the naked ear, once you print the audio waves of the two, they are visually near matches. It's fascinating that two sounds can vary widely on the surface but have the same underlying makeup.

So which word was actually being said? The original recording is of the word *laurel*, with a small overlaid frequency of *yanny* added on top. The word we hear is dependent on the audio wave and pitch we neurologically choose to tune in to. Scientists say this happens almost unconsciously and is dependent on our brain's neurological memory of what we tend to focus on audibly.[2] This focused listening skill is the same mechanism that allows us to focus on our work in a busy coffee shop or allows our spouse to "accidentally" tune us out because the big football game is on TV. How we focus and what we focus on and analyze in the world around us create a subconscious pattern for our auditory systems.

Much more important than being able to distinguish between *yanny* or *laurel* is being able to distinguish the truth among lies. The way we interpret shame matters. It can be the basis of our identity—positively or negatively. That internal processing, the subconscious pattern we create, will determine if shame makes or breaks us.

If shame has been the ringing voice in your head, you may perceive your past to be unequivocally tied to your future. You might tell yourself, *"Well, I messed up once. I'm bound to do it again."* Or *"Why do I think I deserve a healthy relationship? I'm a screwup."* The sounds of shame are communicated through lies.

This deception perception severs the connection we need for learning and growing from our mistakes. Instead, it reworks shame into a continuous loop where we hear the same lines over and over again, feeling stuck in patterns and unsure why we can't break free. Shame keeps us enslaved so we miss out on the freedom of God—not just one day in heaven but even now here on earth. It sounds a false alarm deep within our thoughts and emotions that cries out, "You're guilty! You wicked person, you'll be this way forever!" If that fallacy rings on, it will drown out the true tune of redemption and the beautiful melody of salvation.

I had a friend who'd always tell me *what* she wanted to see different in her life—her confidence, the type of guys she dated, and who she hung out with—but she didn't know *why* she could never actually implement the change. I'd watch as she'd work through the same problems with the same processing each time. Nothing changes externally until we change internally. One day I told her I'd been in her shoes, and I was afraid she hoped for a better future but didn't believe she was worthy of one. After many tears and some laughs, she worked out that she'd been carrying shame from her past. It kept bringing her back to the same patterns. She'd been listening to who her insecurities, fears, and shame told her she was more than who God called her to be. We both agreed she needed to get off that perpetual loop to get where she wanted to be.

When you have the Word in your heart, it will be your source of information and reference. You won't be so easily fooled by shame's misguiding lies because you'll have the truth as a guidepost on your path. You'll see godly fruit in your life when you live from its source. Let's be clear, your shame will not be silenced after a certain amount of time has passed since your biggest mistake or when you finally feel "good enough" to be the person you hope to be. But rather, it's silenced when you tune the words you receive in your heart to be the truth recited from the Word!

The Bible gives us example after example of God's great love, which supersedes anything that could imprison us. He loved you and me at our darkest hour and went to the greatest lengths to override sin and shame!

> Christ arrives right on time to make this happen. He didn't, and doesn't, wait for us to get ready. He presented himself for this sacrificial death when we were far too weak and rebellious to do anything to get ourselves ready. And even if we hadn't been so weak, we wouldn't have known what to do anyway. We can understand someone dying for a person worth dying for, and we can understand how someone good and noble could inspire us to selfless sacrifice. But God put his love on the line for us by offering his Son in sacrificial death while we were of no use whatever to him. (Rom. 5:6–8 MSG)

Not one of us is righteous on our own—not one. Not even the apostle Peter, the martyr James, or your sweet grandma who's an angel on earth. No one earns their virtue on their own. Paul makes this point by saying, "For no one can ever be made right with God by doing what the law commands. The law simply shows us how sinful we are" (Rom. 3:20 NLT).

If you're like me, shame has tried to tell you that your sins and mistakes are far worse than everyone else's and you're damaged goods. But God's been in the redemption business for quite some time now. He's turned murderers into miracle workers and harlots into heroines. Every one of them came to realize they'd fallen short and likely felt the same wave of shame we've dealt with, but they were freed and transformed *from their sins and their shame*. How'd they do it? The trick is knowing how to respond with the knowledge that you've fallen short.

Stop the Shame Game

Shame is no soft word. It's not solely an emotion we feel or prognosis of the past; it's an active infestation in our world that needs to be uprooted.

I first began writing this book because of how overwhelming shame had been in my own life, and I knew I wasn't alone. Many of us have battled lies of shame that kept us from being close to God. I've sat with women whose tears dripped heavy as they lamented the mistakes they'd made and realized how they'd turned those mistakes into secrets as they hid from God, their family, and their friends, inevitably sliding back to what caused their pain in the first place. Every encounter like this breaks my heart. It's a vicious cycle, and the enemy never plays fair.

We need to stop playing the shame game.

It's a losing battle, and the enemy uses isolation as his key tactic. He makes us feel dirty, dirtier than anyone else could understand, and tells us we're all alone in our problems. Somewhere along the way, talking about our hurts or disclosing our wrongdoings was too uncomfortable, so we decided it was better to keep them to ourselves. Could much of the pain we felt from shame have been avoided if we had simply opened up?

When I was at my lowest, battling my most shameful habits and thoughts, the last thing I wanted to do was talk about it or make it public. Keeping it in the dark felt safer than bringing it to the light. I ran from any conversation that would put me close to confessing or processing. I felt I'd be opening Pandora's box if I did. But hauling all that dead weight around gets heavy, far heavier than our human hands can carry. We need a different strategy.

Whenever we're riddled with remorse, opening up may be the last thing we want to do but the best thing we could do.

Flip the narrative and flip the switch. Turn to someone you trust and turn the light on.

Talk it out with a dear friend or trusted mentor. James 5:16 says to confess our sins to one another. Not so they can point fingers but so we can heal. The first time I opened up to some of my closest friends about the shame I was carrying, they were surprised by all I had been keeping to myself. I had battled a slew of emotions alone in the corner when I didn't need to. These friends held my hand, cried with me that night and nights after, and stayed by my side, helping me unload all I'd been bearing. Find friends, family members, or mentors who will walk through this season with you and have your best interests at heart.

If that still feels too scary, let me ask you this: What's at risk and what's to gain? The darkness where shame encamps becomes a haze we need light to see through, even if it seems scary. John 3:20–21 says,

> So the wicked hate the Light and try to hide from it, for the Light fully exposes their lives. But those who love the truth will come into the Light, for the Light will reveal that it was God who produced their fruitful works. (TPT)

Let's break down this verse. I've interpreted *wicked* to mean one who's inherently evil by nature, like the villain in your favorite hero or heroine movie—for example, Ursula in *The Little Mermaid*. But searching the Hebrew translation showed me the meaning was less about being a villain and more synonymous with being a prisoner. The word *wicked* in Hebrew is *rasha`*, meaning "guilty one." With that understanding, we can decipher the reality of our status before Christ—*prisoners* to sin and shame. We're guilty, we pay the price and wear the chains. But He gave us an open door, a get-out-of-jail-free card that isn't confined to a board game. No matter who you are, where you're from, or what you have or haven't done, Jesus made the plea to be your Savior. He holds the key to a life of freedom with a hand stretched through the iron bars—but it's our choice to grasp it. When we hide behind our shame, we are prisoners to its lies. But when we bring our past out of hiding, we encounter promise.

Shame has the power to keep us from heavenly freedom because it imprisons us through lies like these:

"Don't take those keys, you deserve to be here."

"People will only judge you for what you've done!"

"If Jesus was so perfect, how could you ever live like Him after what you've done?"

The enemy wants to keep you tormented. If he can make you think you're too far gone, too dirty, too screwed up to live a life of purpose, then he can

Flip the narrative and flip the switch. Turn to someone you trust and turn the light on.

steal Ethan Hunt's tagline, *"Mission accomplished."* Hiding or ignoring our mistakes keeps us imprisoned. But if we can muster the courage to lay aside the discomfort and vulnerability of opening up, we will find that stepping into the light is cleansing.

I'm a big fan of a bubble bath; it's my favorite way to refresh after a long day. But to enjoy the refreshment and purification it offers, I must first shed my outer layers. It'd be mad to get into bathwater fully clothed—not to mention uncomfortable, I'd imagine. Baths require us to be bare—so does silencing shame.

We trade being covered to be cleansed.

It's worth reiterating here that God isn't trying to expose us like in those past nightmares where we're stark naked in a school auditorium with the harsh stage lights beaming down on us. God's role in the shame game is not trickster or tormentor—**He is the benefactor.** He gave His only Son, the highest form of payment, in exchange for us to walk freely. His light doesn't bash us, it benefits us.

If you're warring with yourself about whether opening up is worth it, remember this: Jesus candidly bore it all, in an exposure full of mistreatment, abandonment, and nakedness, while we merely *feel* those emotions. Remember, you are *never* alone.

There was a woman who had to confront her shame when she came face-to-face with Jesus Himself. The Samaritan woman at the well we read about in John 4 was a robust woman in a sense. Living with her (presumably) soon-to-be sixth husband, she had likely developed some thick skin due to the insults and side-eyes from neighbors and the heartbreak of former loves. The fact that she was performing the laborious task of drawing well water at noon, the solar peak of the day, suggests that she preferred the heat of the sun over her ears burning from the town's gossip.

I doubt this was her only isolated daily event either. She could have had an entire routine planned around avoiding anyone who'd look down on her or make her feel shame. When she met Christ, He broke every social norm she would have expected. Because Jesus was a Jewish man, their race and gender alone should have kept them from even making direct eye contact, let alone associating with each other. Even still, Jesus directly asked the woman for a drink of water.

Taken aback, the woman questioned why and how He was speaking to her. Alluding to His sovereignty, He extended the invitation of eternal life to her and she asked to receive the gift. But, knowing her situation, He responded, "Go, call your husband and come back" (v. 16). But why? Was it to embarrass her? Or to partake in the town bullying to see how she'd respond? Again—Jesus is always intentional. She didn't become offended or get up and leave; instead, she started to believe. This encounter is told through a brief recounting, only taking up verses 7–42. If we skim the lines, we can misinterpret or miss the significance. Jesus could come across as curt or rude, commanding and shaming this woman because of her past. But like much of the Bible, we must read unhurriedly and expectantly.

Christ was illuminating the area she'd kept hidden that was in turn making her hide from others. Going through life without properly dealing with shame keeps a wound exposed. This woman's very way of living, down to her mundane daily tasks, was presumably altered by the shame she felt. Instead of coping with or overcoming what she'd done in the past, she continued moving in the same direction while shame acted as a bumper, keeping her from changing course.

Some might imagine that with God being good and loving, Jesus would give her one of those "There, there, it's all okay. You are loved!" big-brother talks. In my opinion, that's the worst way we can respond to shame. It's comparable to the friend who says you look great but fails to tell you there's actually a piece of lettuce stuck between your teeth so they don't embarrass you. Avoiding the awkward or uncomfortable isn't beneficial for anyone. We need to confront what is ill-fit in our lives. No one wants to walk around with lettuce in their teeth, and they would feel humiliated when they finally saw for themselves what was evident all along. Would you rather your friend or a group of strangers point it out?

Jesus acted in the woman's best interest. He took one look at her and said (figuratively), "Lady, you've got a lot going for you, but there's some lettuce in your teeth we've got to get out first." Christ always goes after His bride—even when it's uncomfortable, uncommon, or incomprehensible. If there's anything standing between us and the freedom He offers us, He confronts it. He declared as much boldly on the cross. Out of love, He refuses to let us walk around unknowingly wearing something out of place, be it food in our teeth or shame in our head. The Samaritan woman couldn't see herself as a daughter of God until she threw out everything, past or present, that competed with the identity Jesus had waiting for her.

See, shame doesn't treat us softly, so we shouldn't treat it that way either. We need to go after it, get real, and give that breakup closure. My theory is that Jesus knew how this Samaritan woman saw herself and knew she needed a spark of truth and a glimpse of life-changing power. When he told her to go call her husband, she responded, "I have no husband" (v. 17). Technically she was telling the truth because she had only *ex-husbands*, but sensing what she aimed to suppress and the shame tethered to it, Jesus shared that He knew of her past and invited her to live differently—not because of her past but because of the prophesies about the Messiah.

She was the first person Jesus openly told that He was the Son of God. Why would He choose to first disclose the greatest identity proclamation in all of history to this *shameful* foreign woman? A generation gasped when Darth Vader dropped the iconic line "I am your father."[3] Being the avid *Star Wars* fan he is, my husband reminds me how pivotal this revelation was and how it's part of what makes the series legendary. How much more shocking and awe-inspiring was Christ's confession? And how special the ears that first heard it from the source!

Jesus often operated in the unexpected and through the unassuming. He used a seemingly small moment to revive a woman worn down by the years of her youth. He used that broken woman to break racial tensions and spread revival. On that day, she walked to the well isolated by shame but left fueled by faith.

> Then, leaving her water jar, the woman went back to the town and said to the people, "Come, see a man who told me everything I ever did. Could this be the Messiah?" They came out of the town and made their way toward him. . . . Many of the Samaritans from that town believed in him because of the woman's testimony, "He told me everything I ever did." So when the Samaritans came to him, they urged him to stay with them, and he stayed two days. And because of his words many more became believers. (John 4:28–30; 39–41)

What can change in your life through one honest encounter with Christ? What ways has shame kept you from experiencing a miraculous breakthrough? Believe, confront, and repent.

Admit and Repent

How have you coped with shame in the past? Did you try one of the common methods: going out, numbing the pain, hooking up, or ignoring your feelings? All these approaches bury what needs to be worked through or heap on even more shame. I'm not saying it's fun or easy to work through these emotions, but it is necessary, unpleasant as it may feel at first. A flower doesn't grow until the dirt has been worked through and the seed planted.

When Adam and Eve were in the garden of Eden, they lived in a luxurious and fruitful habitat, had more than they could ever want, and best of all, actually walked with God. Yet, as the story goes, despite their ideal situation, they still sinned. The Bible says that after they ate the fruit from the tree of the knowledge of good and evil, they were ashamed of their nakedness and covered themselves with fig leaves (Gen. 3:7).

That's the funny thing about shame; even though Adam and Eve were naked and were man and wife, permitting them to see each other in an intimate state, their shame drove them to the point of hiding. It can do the same for us. We feel less than deserving of God's goodness, so we try to hide our sin, or even ourselves, from Him.

Shame is one of the enemy's sneakiest tactics, because, in part, its message is true—we have fallen short and do not deserve a do-over. But what shame fails to remember is that while we were still sinners, Christ died for us (Rom. 5:8).

We need to release any misconstrued mindsets or broken definitions of grace to effectively silence shame. For example, some people would say grace is just a covering for what we've done. But if grace were only a covering of sin, that would mean our shame remains, buried beneath anything good we produce after the fact. But grace doesn't cover our shame; it eradicates it entirely.

The Bible says, "As far as the east is from the west, so far does he remove our transgressions from us" (Ps. 103:12 ESV). That means adios, shame—good riddance, see ya never! It also means we don't work toward our good standing with Christ, as if some of us are "worthy" of heaven and others are too far gone.

Because it's bigger than we are. Grace is one thing we cannot work out ourselves. We can't do enough, pray enough, or be enough to earn it. It's our gift from God. We can apply ourselves, focus our attention, and learn new skills (as you are doing now with this book), but only He who knew no sin can remove ours and the effects that follow it. This doesn't mean we shouldn't strive to live a God-honoring life or continually work at being our best. It simply means we have to tie our good works to something bigger than ourselves.

We come to the point of repentance because we realize we are only humans, but where we choose to go from there is up to us. Will you choose shame, which leaves you wounded and stagnant? Or will you choose grace, which leads to faith and life?

Choosing shame over grace is the equivalent of telling God all He did on the cross was for nothing. The truth is, when Christ defeated sin that day, He defeated the effects of sin too: regret, pain, and shame. God is currently doing a good work in your life, but if you listen to the lies of shame, you'll be choking out the good seeds from growing and watering the weeds instead.

Live Unashamed

There's no mute button to silence shame. It takes smashing the radio and destroying the static to get the noise out of our lives. And trust me, I get it. The first time Arden and I went back to visit Alabama during our first year of marriage, shame swept over me about who I'd been before and the things I'd done. As we passed places connected to painful memories, I was instantly transported back to the girl I used to be.

Arden was my husband. He knew me deeply and intimately. We lived together, worked together, and led together in ministry. But during that trip, I didn't want him to even look at me, and I felt the least qualified to lead anyone. Those memories resurfacing were an attack on my future! My old stomping grounds brought up old spiritual ground I hadn't yet conquered. I'd allowed the enemy to still have territory over me through shame. "For whatever overcomes a person, to that he is enslaved" (2 Pet. 2:19 ESV). You have to overcome what once overcame you, knowing the past doesn't define you because you're no longer the same person.

I was uncomfortable in my past home because it reminded me of my past mistakes. Being back there made me fear those old mistakes would resurface, but as God and my husband reassured me, I was in fact a new creation in Him. But I had to walk in that surety, even as thoughts of my past failures and pains came back to mind like a tornado ravaging through my peace. This is why silencing shame needs to be a clean break. Otherwise, it'll pull the classic ex move and reach out just when you least expect it or are finally moving on. During that trip, I asked God for a way to proclaim the victory He'd given me, to release the grip those past places and memories held on me. He led me to a declaration that changed my mindset and established a confidence in me that lasts to this day:

> Instead of your shame
>   you will receive a double portion,
> and instead of disgrace
>   you will rejoice in your inheritance.
> And so you will inherit a double portion in your land,
>   and everlasting joy will be yours. (Isa. 61:7)

The truth of the Word is a shame silencer. It puts our broken mindset to rest and awakens blessing. After reading this verse from Isaiah, I was overcome with undeniable joy. I could see the truth so clearly! Why was I letting this reminder of who I once was pull me back when it should launch me forward? In remembering those past mistakes, I was reminded of how much God had saved me from and what great lengths He went to save a lost child. When He saved me, I repented and was released from my past mistakes.

Why had I allowed these memories to make me ashamed and cause me to shrink back when I should have boasted all the louder? I could rejoice in my inheritance because I knew I was no longer my old self. I was a daughter of God!

It was a double-portion blessing to experience His great love, which saved me when I couldn't save myself, and to know I am His redeemed. We can silence shame by awakening this double-portion blessing of gratitude and belonging. Repentance that leads to gratitude is a two-edged sword. We fight the binds that try to pull us back to sin and rebuke the shame that wants to keep us from moving forward. Such a blessing is a celebration where the enemy is expecting lamentation!

When we trade our shame for His mercy, we have space to receive two times more than we could formerly hold. We have both the blessing of knowing God's sovereign love that rescued us from our sin and shame, yet we also have the blessing of a testimony that will help us reach others who find themselves where we once were.

Moments are just ripples in time unless they're connected to something greater that causes them to become tidal waves. To make a powerful impact, our lives need purpose. The moments you've experienced shame, regret, and fear, the enemy purposed to tear you down, to break your heart and your spirit. But those memories that felt like a storm tossing you to and fro are forced to submit to the purpose God has for your life. They dwindle to ripples as He takes what the enemy meant for evil and turns it to work for good.

Our God isn't a tyrant king who seeks ways to punish us for our mistakes. He's a loving God who looks past who we've been and invites us to a new future. But this future is no cute nickname He gives us or a Band-Aid for what we've walked through. It's a lifelong, life-changing relationship with Him. We must break up with those toxic relationships—comparison, regret, anxiety, shame—to fully begin our lifetime with Christ. We cannot have split personalities when it comes to redemption—are we ashamed or redeemed?

As we move forward, we can be unashamed and unaffected by our former mistakes because we're confident in our new identity as daughters of God. He healed my heart, gave me a new future, and set my feet on solid ground. Once we embrace who we are in Him, we can break up with who we used to be.

To the girl I was in the past, I forgive you.

Now it's your turn! You can forgive who you used to be because God has forgiven you. Lighten the load and walk into your future. Regret and shame have no residence where you are going! Forgive the girl you used to be—the one who messed up and fell short. You cannot change the past, but you can release it. I want you to throw off the shackles of shame so you can experience healing, life-transforming love, and freedom.

To break up with shame, you need to:

1. Listen closely.
2. Stop the shame game.
3. Admit and repent.
4. Live unashamed.

Remember, instead of our shame—and the pain, worry, and angst that come from it—we will have a double-portion blessing. When we place our faith in God, we see these moments attach to His grand plan and become a tidal wave He uses to wash us clean.

Little did we know that in all these broken moments we've discussed, we weren't drowning, but we were learning to swim.

THE
BREAK
AWAY

Part 2

Prepare the land.

Forsake the old and welcome the new,
seek His face and behold what He brings you to.

God has assembled a sanctuary for His people,
a storehouse never-ending for those in His temple.

The wilderness will be glad and rejoice,
the barren season rejuvenated—lush and ready.
Dead bones come alive at the sound of His voice.
Alone? Impossible. With Him? On the contrary.

The days of torment and toil have ceased,
your heart and mind now rest at ease.

Your steps redeemed and anointed with oil.
The desert becomes fertile; the dirt becomes soil.

You are birthing.
You are resurrecting.
You are establishing.
You are metamorphosing.

As the lilies grow from the richness of the Lord's hands,
break away from the past and watch how your life expands.

06. The Broken Myth of "Enough"

> We often block our own blessings because we don't feel inherently good enough or smart enough or pretty enough or worthy enough.
>
> —Oprah Winfrey

A number of fables we heard growing up were based on real-life people. Granted, Disney added the pixie dust and fairy godmothers, but behind many of these fictitious heroines were real women with fascinating stories.

Take Rapunzel, for example. She was based on a young woman named Barbara who lived in Italy in the third century. She didn't have hair a mile long, but she did have notable beauty that drew the attention of many suitors. There was no evil witch who was jealous of her youth, but her father was stern and concerned about her looks. He was set on choosing the man she would marry. Being a traveling merchant, he became concerned Barbara would marry someone he didn't approve of while he was away. How could he "protect" his young daughter while he was gone? You guessed it—he hid her away in a tower.[1]

I get wanting to protect your daughter and steer her in the right direction, but this was over-the-top. Apparently he even hired a group of men to watch her and make sure she stayed put.

Can you imagine what Barbara went through locked away high above the world around her? The isolation, frustration, and boredom would have been insufferable, but the betrayal of her loved one would have been devastating. What gets me the most is that while we grew up picturing the villainous witch sending Rapunzel to her confinement, lo and behold, it was her own father. Dad, if you read this, thank you for not locking me in a cold concrete building. I really appreciate that!

While I truly pray you never find yourself tucked away in a forsaken fortress, your life could still share some similarities with Barbara's story. You may not be locked in a physical tower, but you might be locked in a mental one—the fortress of *Am I Enough?*

Many of us have built this, block by block, by stacking our accomplishments and ideologies. It's a tall, tall tower we can't seem to break out of. Fortified and skyscraping, it casts a shadow on our plans and potential. Anytime we lack or stumble in an area, we think, *I'll never be ___ enough.* Wham! Another brick piled up. Higher and higher the barrier gets until we're trapped—enclosed by this monument dedicated to reminding us we just don't have what it takes.

You get the picture.

We're constantly striving to be better, look better, do better. How many of us have been that girl staring at the mirror, thinking, *Is my skin clear* enough? *Are my lashes long* enough? *Am I smart* enough *to get this job? Will I be* enough *for him to stay?*

In my own life, entertaining the broken idea of "enough" only led to questioning everything I was and all I had to offer. Until we break up with the myth of being "enough," we will be building an isolating life. It's time for that wall to come crumbling down so we can see clearly how to build our lives according to God's standards! And I've got four breakup moves to get you started.

Put Down the Phone

Wait, did you feel that? Your phone just vibrated, didn't it? Did you just check it now?

Don't worry, we've all done it—felt a familiar buzz in our pocket or purse, but for some reason the text didn't appear. This is a phenomenon called "Phantom Pocket Vibration Syndrome." If you've experienced this sensation, congratulations, you're not crazy or alone! Dr. Michelle Drouin was curious how many of her undergraduates had felt this false alarm and found 89 percent of her students experienced it roughly every two weeks.[2] So what gives? Are our phones faulty, or are we becoming faulty from using them?

A Nokia study found that the average person checks their cell phone every six and a half minutes or 150 times per day.[3] That's startling. I wish I was doing something truly beneficial that often— rather than tapping a screen—like reading my Bible, telling loved ones how much they mean to me, or doing an ab workout (maybe then I'd finally get that six-pack). Every six and a half minutes in a day . . . that's a large chunk of our lives to give to anything, let alone a device. It suggests this question: Are we obsessed with these tiny technological squares in our pockets or is it the "vibes" they give us?

When you eat candy, you get a sugar rush. When you get a text, you get a hit of dopamine.[4] Dopamine is a reward neurotransmitter—a chemical that essentially tells your body, "Hey, this is nice. I like it!" We *like* to receive texts. We *like* to feel wanted. We *like* to be thought of, especially positively. Anyone who's ever received that "I was just thinking of you" text knows exactly how powerful that dopamine hit can be. This feel-good rush is one big reason behind our need to constantly keep our cell phones close. We crave that affirmation or proof that we matter and desire an alert or sign that something is going on or someone needs us.

It becomes like a drug. The hit of dopamine we feel when we receive a text message, social media notification, or email (for us millennials and older) comforts us when we're fighting inner battles. When we're uncertain about who we are and if we matter, we tend to turn to tangible things because they're instantly gratifying. Those messages drown our doubt—at least for a little while.

But it's a temporary antidote—a partial masking more than a true medicine. We will never reach wholeness by depending on distractions such as these.

See a Doctor

Back when my relationship with Arden was still new, I traveled with Lisa for the first time to a conference. I was determined to get to know her better and show her that her baby boy was marrying the right girl! But I also had an aching, itchy throat. Talk about inopportune timing. I didn't have much time before I needed to head out, and I was not going to mess up this trip, so I did what any reasonable lady would do in my position—I went to Starbucks instead of to the doctor.

"Grab a hot tea and get it together!" was my inner rally. So I got their Medicine Ball tea (look it up next time you're sick—you're welcome) and hit the road. Each day of the trip, my symptoms got worse. I started popping cough drops like candy so I could keep up with the weekend's events and told myself that my raspy voice was fun and sexy, not frustrating and stifling. Four days later, the conference ended, and I woke up the following morning having nearly lost my ability to swallow and feeling like I had golf balls for lymph nodes—okay, not fun or sexy at all.

It was time to get back to reality and past time to visit a doctor. After an uncomfortable throat swab, the doctor returned and said, "Ma'am, you have strep throat." Oh, well, that sure explained my symptoms! Once I knew what I was suffering from, I got the right medicine (not just a Starbucks drink) and started feeling better the very next day.

I could have made time to get a proper diagnosis before the trip so that I wouldn't have had to smile despite an extremely sore throat for four days. If we're in a rush to skip the assessment, we'll convince ourselves it's not that bad, that we just need to put on our big-girl britches and keep moving. But we won't get much better just putting on a smile.

If you're carrying a generational ailment—an insecurity from childhood or a hard-hitting personal pain point—you need what the doctor ordered. Soothing the symptoms will only make you feel better for a little while. Validation and affirmation are the Medicine Ball and cough drops we use when we long to be enough.

You must choose what your aid will be: a substance or sustenance? Will you turn to one more text, hit, or hookup, or will you turn to *the* One?

My achy breaky throat needed saving. So did my inner critic; the little heartbroken girl trying to be enough. The one who admits their faults and walks into the examination room is braver and closer to healing than someone who does not. I can be confident in who I am, despite my limitations and flaws, because I know that when God redeems them, they become a chance to glorify the Savior (2 Cor. 12:9).

To truly treat a problem, we need an accurate diagnosis. Like with any real ailment, we need testing and examination to discover what's occurring under the surface.

I was raised with a healthy idea of who I could be in Christ. I loved Jesus for saving and seeing me, because, frankly, I longed to be seen. But God was far away, and the things of the world felt much closer and more comforting. That mindset infected my entire outlook and affected my actions and intentions.

I can remember going to places, dressing certain ways, and doing things I didn't want to do all for the sake of being accepted. I was silently screaming "love me!" to anyone who would listen. Honestly, after I was married, I had a hard time pinning down why I had dated some of the guys I did in the past. When I reflected on my choices, I realized why: they noticed me. They say people drink excessively most often when they're trying to numb their pain. I get that . . . I became intoxicated by attention as I tried to anesthetize my insecurities and feelings of inferiority.

When you think about it, the effects of alcohol and attention-seeking are not that different from each other. This attention intoxication deceives us with blurred vision and slurred speech. We perceive the world around us through a different lens and say things that don't sound like us. I assume a hangover from binge drinking would have quite the repercussions, but I know for a fact that the hangover from getting buzzed off others' opinions and validation was nauseating. We must get sober to rid our bodies of the damages of alcohol, and we must become sober-minded to rid ourselves of the dangers of getting our worth from others.

A little appreciation from our peers or a celebration of our hard work isn't bad, but if we're getting lost in or high off validation, it needs to be addressed. It numbs what's decaying inside of us. A mixed drink can't fix our longings any more than a compliment can heal our brokenness. That's why we need to see a doctor—to properly treat the problem.

God is our doctor. He knows what's hurting and how to fix it. The Bible says, "For he satisfies the longing soul, and the hungry soul he fills with good things" (Ps. 107:9 ESV). Mary, the mother of Jesus, chased after God, and He put a blessing in her that only He could do with someone hungry for Him alone. She cried out, "He [God] has filled the hungry with good things" (Luke 1:53 ESV). Our appetite for God's good things will not leave us wanting more. Choosing sustenance over substance leads to satiety. God will satisfy us in Him. We become whole when we wholeheartedly put our identity and hope in Christ.

Follow the Leader

If you are one of those people who always picks up loose trash while helping someone cross the street, after you prayed for the barista who got your eight-dollar coffee order horribly wrong even though you paid for it and the person behind you, then please, come be my friend and rub off on me! But even if you live like the good Samaritan, your kind gestures aren't the only attribute God is looking for.

The Word teaches us that our good works don't save us or make us "good." Our faith in Christ, His transformation of our minds, and the submission of our flaws to Him are most important. That's why Paul could both confidently speak of his transformed, righteous state after his encounter with Christ and remind himself and his readers that, in his words, he was "the least of the apostles" (1 Cor. 15:9 ESV).

What I'm getting at here is that if we aim to become "good enough," we will be equally disappointed in ourselves for missing the mark and hopelessly lost in our search for freedom and joy. Hyperfocusing on our image or accolades leads to shame because we idolize an ideal version of ourselves rather than looking to Jesus. No version of ourselves that we could imagine can reach that pinnacle of perfection, because we were not made to be enough in that regard. Hebrews 12:1–2 exhorts us to look to Jesus because He both originated and perfected faith, two things no other human being can do.

Don't let this discourage you though! As in everything, there's a logical reason we miss the mark. It's so that no man or woman can boast in their own successes or be diminished by their own failures. For as many times as I do get it right, respond correctly, and love my neighbor, I equally get it wrong, become impatient, and must ask forgiveness at the end of the day.

And don't let this demotivate you from doing good either! For while we *don't* chase after our own perfected image, we *do* chase after the perfect One. The verse in Hebrews 12 says *run*! Run the race set out before you. Like an athlete in a baton relay, we can see our Savior ahead of us urging us not to slow down but rather to speed up! First John 2:29 and 2 Timothy 2:22, respectively, urge us to both practice and pursue righteousness. There's something graciously beautiful about God constantly urging us to keep going forward with a mercy that allows for error while we grow.

We're like a child perpetually learning to ride a bicycle without training wheels. We can get frustrated that we can't simply hop on and go, boasting in our ability and unbound in our freedom.

Or better yet, we can keep our eyes ahead and see the Father who is backpedaling ahead of us, cheering us on with abounding love and guiding us with the greatest smile on His face. I believe that same abounding love is what led God to decide that we humans shouldn't arrive at that measure of enough here on this earth. Will you trust in that with me and allow it to release and strengthen you?

> Let me hear Your lovingkindness in the morning,
> For I trust in You.
> Teach me the way in which I should walk,
> For I lift up my soul to You. (Ps. 143:8 AMP)

God knew we would fall short as humans. That's why He sent His Son to make up for what we lack. He doesn't ask us to be perfect; He asks something better instead: "Follow me" (Matt. 4:19). Following God instead of chasing our own deity will take us farther, keep us grounded, and sustain us longer.

Accept the Limit

"Enough is enough" until it isn't.

Though we constantly search for it, there is no measure of "enough." If we are hoping to reach a magic number or a top tier of approval from those around us, we will be searching with no end. Surprisingly, we can garner wisdom about this topic from a movie I never thought I'd use for a plausible life lesson: *Mean Girls*. In the final scenes of the movie, Cady Heron is competing in a Mathletes competition for North Shore High School. The sudden-death question she's picked to solve involves finding the limit of a fraction. As she works through the problem on the board and the problems in her life, she's enlightened to the fundamental truth that self-worth cannot be found in the rise and fall of others' opinions or striving to be someone we're not. Self-confidence comes only by facing life's problems head-on. In full convergence, this realization leads her to solve the mathematical problem facing her. In victorious triumph, she shouts, "The limit does not exist!"[5]

The measure to "enough" increases without bound—there is always another tier to reach, another person's approval to gain, or another year to magically stop aging. The limit to where these "good enough" lines run is limitless. There are infinite ways we can measure ourselves, but they're all in vain. We must then eradicate "enough" from our vocabulary when it comes to our self-worth.

It's not about becoming enough; it's about being enough.

God has gifted us with characteristics, talents, and sentiments all sufficiently supplied how He deems fit. If there is no measure of enough, then we will never arrive at its end; we must abandon that tower we're building completely.

We are finite females by nature. The worldly scale we measure ourselves by will keep us falling short. All the while, we are enough to God. It's an oxymoron, really. Not being enough means we are enough. The way God loves us forsakes worldly measure. It's not about *becoming* enough; it's about *being* enough. When we're striving to become something or someone, we're looking to what the world says is worthy or important. But when we join our hearts with God's, we find the togetherness that will unite us to who we are deep inside.

This idea of *being* enough is synonymous with peace and rest rather than striving and perfecting. Christ doesn't measure us in a linear pattern. He doesn't require us to level up enough before He loves us. We'll never hear Him say, "Ouch, sorry. You didn't make it to the top tier? No kingdom rewards for you!" No, God gives us a first-class, one-way ticket to His throne room and offers us a better title than we could ever pine and jockey for by ourselves: cherished daughters. This adoption means He sees us, flaws and all, and declares us royalty by bestowing His majesty on us. He extends an eternal invitation to forsake living by our own futile measuring stick.

Let us then approach God's throne of grace with confidence, so that we may receive mercy and find grace to help us in our time of need. (Heb. 4:16)

I know it's a cliché that every little girl fantasizes about being a princess, and maybe growing up with Disney classics did influence my imagination, but there's something about the comparison of being in the likeness of royalty that shows how lofty the Father's love for us is. As God's royal heirs and Christ's bride whom he died for, we have what the stories and movies depict—the honor of being loved, seen, and chosen. The things you set your heart on await you already. From the beginning God loved you; He made you and selected you. To Him, you've always been enough.

Considering such love, do your old ways of measuring yourself carry much merit now? There are no point systems or scorecards in eternity. Toss those old formulas and frameworks out of your mind like the high school trigonometry you ditched right after you took your finals. Human beings have limits, but God doesn't. Evangelist and minister Billy Graham challenged a generation to shift their focus, saying, "What really matters is how God sees me. He isn't concerned with labels; He is concerned about the state of man's soul. . . . Because of the saving grace Jesus has extended to me, and my repentance of sin, I am His child."[6]

I hear Graham's words as an invitation to forsake the boxes we find ourselves in—professionally, socially, and religiously—and focus on the One (Christ) we've been found in instead.

If you'd say something of this nature—*I believe God is kind and good, but I doubt He could do anything significant through me*—let me shine some light on such thinking with this hard truth: God showcased His glory through kings, angels, and mountains, but He also used donkeys (Mark 11:1–11), sticks (Exod. 7:8–13), and dirt (John 8:1–11). He can use you on your best *and* your worst days.

Don't limit what God does on this earth by focusing on what you perceive to be your limitations. He does some of His best work through the most common creations. And He sees you as much more precious than any of these things. Your insecurities and inabilities do not hinder what God can and readily wants to do for and through you. The sacrifice of His Son shows that, to Him, you are worthy.

It's possible for God to do a mighty work in you even if you feel feeble. It's possible for Him to multiply the gifts and talents you have now to an astounding degree. And it's possible for you to operate from a place of wholeness. You don't need a certain award, title, or distinction; you only need to intimately know the distinguishing factors He placed in you.

Trust Your Investor

At the end of the day, we can't cash in on what anyone else did with their twenty-four hours—we can only claim our own. So don't waste time worrying about how much someone else is making, how successful your friend's start-up seems, or how the latest beauty influencer's skin appears to be acne free 24/7. What creates possibility within your life is leaning into what God placed within you. Relieve yourself from fixating on others' capabilities and you'll allow the space needed to discover your own capacity.

Once you understand that you don't work for your standing, you can begin to thrive in your talents—your God-given talents. The parable of the talents in Matthew 25 shows that while your giftings are not measured in quantity, they are observed in quality of care. God did not form you without purpose. You're neither a duplicate nor disposable—you are by design. By debunking the myth of "enough," you gain the ability to see clearly how He created you and what He created you for.

Think of God as your heavenly investor.

Business owners rely on investors for many reasons—monetary aid, vital expertise, and systematic support. Entrepreneurs are often passionate and want to make a difference. Their investors can help them refocus if they get overly ambitious about where the business should be or too worried about a competitor's numbers.

The business owner who partners with a venture capitalist typically achieves success at a faster and greater rate than those who venture out on their own.

God sees your life, your plans, and your dreams and says, "I believe in you enough to bet on you." He faithfully footed the bill and put down equity before any evidence of fulfillment. He believes in your success because He's in it with you.

To break up with the broken myth of enough, you need to:

1. Put down the phone.
2. See a doctor.
3. Accept the limit.
4. Trust your investor.

You may be wondering, *Hey, what happened to that real-life Rapunzel from earlier?* The story goes that while her father was away, Barbara discovered a freedom that penetrated the walls surrounding her. Somehow, she found a Bible and fell in love with Christ, devoting herself to the faith. In the third century, Christianity was forbidden in Italy. When her father returned from his trip and found out about her conversion, he was furious and led her to the authorities and ultimately to her death. Some accounts claim God granted her an escape, while others say her father was struck down by lightning. Much is still unknown about this woman, but we know that the Word came to her even in her captivity.

She is now known as Saint Barbara, admired and considered a martyr for her faith.[7] Freedom in a world of captivity can only come from God.

God offers us talents, protection, family, authority, healing, and promises that are *more than enough*. The next time we feel we aren't adequate, we can remember that He is. We can trust that His view and position in our lives are more profound and profitable than even our own.

07. Liar, Liar

> Beyond a doubt truth bears the same relation to falsehood as light to darkness.
>
> —Leonardo da Vinci

The world is good at lying to women, isn't it? From the time we're born, we're fed lies so subtly that we slowly lose the ability to recognize them. We build blinders to truth as we are conditioned to see through a worldly lens. We believe lies about our appearance, purpose, and identity, such as these:

"You're too thin" or "You're too curvy."

"You don't have anything to offer."

"You'll never be happy without___."

Magazines sell us the idea that we must mirror photoshopped supermodels to be accepted as beautiful. Feminism shouts that we can only get power by taking it from men. Beauty companies oversell our need for the next top-of-the-line product and understate the negative, or lack of, results. These are just a few of the lies women face.

We've grown up under the false pretense that something is innately wrong with us, who we are isn't good enough, and who we want to be is out of the question. We're told that to be truly complete, to be desirable, we must find an external solution—that all the answers to our issues can be obtained from the world rather than found within.

So, what do we do? We buy the latest workout programs and face creams promoting the magic cure for our insecurities and problems. We search for a partner, or even just a companion, everywhere we go—at work, at school, even in elevators. But the truth is, no matter how much we work out, how many creams we buy, or how many dates we go on, we will never satisfy the longings that these lies place inside us using the solutions they propose. Because the world offers persistent problems but short-term solutions.

So why exactly are we so eager to believe the lies others tell us about who we are or who we should be? I'm afraid that, too many times, we give in to believing lies because of what we hope to gain. We want to be loved, seen, and chosen. We want to do whatever makes us feel good and forget what hurts. So when someone points out that we are missing something, instead of standing firm in the truth that we are already whole, we let the lie tell us what we need and set out to find the antidote that will make us better. We hand over our peace of mind and sense of self, thinking we will get something better in return. We spend all our money on "miracle" products, skip meals to feel thin, and give all of ourselves for just one night to feel "chosen."

> *Too many times, we give in to believing lies because of what we hope to gain.*

But what happens when the curtains open to show nothing but smoke and mirrors? When we think we're following our hearts but realize we've been let down? When we bet it all but are left with nothing but empty pockets? When we wholeheartedly believe we're doing the right thing, but it all collapses in front of us? What do we do then? When we realize we bought into a lie, it's time to get a refund.

We can repurpose that pain. We can restore the right beliefs. We can resurrect our innocence and rediscover our value. We don't have to be shackled to the pain we felt; we can become victors over the lies. God wants to rewrite every lie we've believed with a truth He's proclaimed.

When we allow God to expose the deceptions we've lived under, three things happen: we remove strongholds and are able to grow in righteousness; we stop putting our faith in this world and put it back in God; and we see ourselves and the path set out in front of us more clearly.

In this chapter, I want you to pinpoint the personal lies you've fallen for and find the right path to healing. As you process the different lies you've believed, you will feel a weight released as you are no longer gripped by them. Remember, the deeper you go in these chapters, the more you'll get. I encourage you to see yourself in the stories and ask God to expose any lies you've been living under. He can and will—if you allow Him to. The lies we face, some common for us all as women and others individually spoken, are no match for the never-changing truth. We should feel the freedom to breathe easy, lay it all out on the table, and compare what we've believed to what the Word of God says.

Exposing the lies will require us to drop our guards. As we progress, keep this in mind: some lies will easily reveal themselves as destructive, while others may try harder to cling to the facade that they're true. I've found the lies that say "You are not _____" are the easiest to distinguish, while the lies with the message "You are _____" are generally harder to pick out. We're going to tackle both now and address three lies in each category. Let's start with "You are not _____" lies.

The Lies: "You Are Not" Statements

I've recently detected a commonality in success stories. It's what I like to call the "overcomer element." Many entrepreneurs and creators, such as Albert Einstein, Maya Angelou, and Walt Disney, overcame either verbal or physical disadvantages or abuse and rose to their true potential and identity. Einstein was mute during childhood and labeled "dumb," yet he went on to be a brilliant physicist. Angelou also went mute as a post-trauma symptom of being raped as a child, but she later used her voice to share her journey and create a life of humor, cheer, and compassion. Disney was fired from his first job and told he lacked imagination and creativity, but his imagination later fueled a legacy that would foster joy for decades. These people all faced external and internal lies that they were "not"—not smart, not brave, and not creative. But each of these successful people threw off these lies about what they weren't and, in turn, discovered who they were.

Maybe you, too, have had someone or something tell you what you were not. Perhaps an aptitude test placed you at the bottom of the class or a former coach or teacher said you didn't have what it takes or the MASH game you played in middle school said you'd become a spinster and live in a shack, and you never quite got over it. These "are not" lies pick at a weakness, insecurity, or circumstance and say we are not greater than them. They tell us who we are by trying to say what we are not.

Our enemy doesn't have to beat us; he just has to beat us down. He wants to make us unaware of the assets we have by God's authority. It's one of the oldest tricks in the book. In the famous ancient publication *The Art of War*, Sun Tzu, a fourth-century Chinese general, strategist, and philosopher, said, "All warfare is based on deception."[1] If that's Satan's MO, then we must become undeceivable.

It stirs something within us when we hear stories of those who have walked through a similar situation to what we may be facing and came out shining on the other side. A biblical hero who overcame many "are not" lies is David. From shepherd boy to king, moral failure to faithful, this man shows us that we become triumphant when we overcome lies and walk in truth. The following are three lies that you and I, like David, must overcome if we are to be undeceivable.

Lie #1: You Are Not Special

When a prophet named Samuel was sent by God to anoint the next mighty king of Israel, he was instructed to go to the house of Jesse (David's father) and find the next king among his sons.

There was another king on the throne at the time, King Saul, who had become a dishonorable leader by putting his own agenda before God's. In that time, a king would rule until his death, then his eldest male heir would be the next in line to the throne. Because of this, Samuel's quest for a new king outside the palace while the king was still alive was quite controversial, so he knew he had to 1) make the trip under false pretenses, and 2) be completely Spirit-led in his pursuit and sure of who he chose. To avoid raising suspicion, Samuel traveled to town and met the governing elders under the guise of performing a sacrifice. Once there, he invited Jesse and his sons to the event so he could safely meet with them. When Jesse and seven of his sons arrived, Samuel studied the sons and asked God which was the next king. The Bible conveys that to Samuel's delight, the sons were mighty and pleasing in appearance. Right away he thought the first son presented to him, Eliab, was surely the chosen one because he seemed like a king from head to toe.

> When they arrived, Samuel saw Eliab and thought, "Surely the LORD's anointed stands here before the LORD." (1 Sam. 16:6)

I imagine in this moment that Samuel was thinking he had the crème de la crème before him, and Jesse was standing tall watching his sons be admired. But despite the two men's delight, God disagreed . . . verbally.

> But the LORD said to Samuel, "Do not consider his appearance or his height, for I have rejected him. The LORD does not look at the things people look at. People look at the outward appearance, but the LORD looks at the heart." (v. 7)

One by one, Samuel studied Jesse's sons and thought they seemed to fit the bill, but God kept saying no. Of the seven sons presented, none were chosen. So, a surely puzzled Samuel asked Jesse if these were all his sons. Jesse replied that his youngest son was back tending the sheep. Then Samuel boldly responded, "Send for him; we will not sit down until he arrives" (v. 11).

Jesse's decision separated his sons into two categories: the seven who were fit to be king and the one who was only a shepherd boy. The Bible doesn't give us the backstory to Jesse's thinking process. It could have been unintentional or calculated, but either way, Jesse's decision to leave David behind communicated the message that David was not special enough in his father's eyes.

Whether it was that David wasn't old, strong, or important enough to come, I have to imagine if you or I were David in this situation, we would feel the weight of being left behind. Maybe you've been in a situation where you were unintentionally or consciously left behind. Such a situation can sting and seep into our minds, especially if we place our identity in others' opinions or validations.

When David arrived on the scene to meet his family and the prophet, the Lord spoke again. With one look at the young shepherd, Samuel heard God say, "Rise and anoint him; this is the one" (v. 12). Samuel anointed David as the next king in front of his father and brothers, those who had left him behind, and the Bible says from that day on, David walked mightily in the spirit of the Lord (v. 13). The young boy who was not enough for his earthly father was enough for his heavenly Father.

The time between when David was left behind and when Samuel anointed him was short in hindsight, but even in that quick duration he could have bought into the lie that he wasn't special. It's easy to take rejection or being overlooked or forgotten to heart. But when we do, we let the disease of that lie tie us up with sorrow. If we believe we're not special, we will lose sight of our purpose, our identity, and the way God loves us.

Thankfully David didn't buy into the lie. We can take away that David was not diminished in any way by being left behind; he remained radiant. Upon his arrival to meet Samuel, the Bible says, "He was glowing with health and had a fine appearance and handsome features" (v. 12). This was a confident man walking by the Spirit.

While Jesse and his seven sons awaited confirmation that wouldn't come, David tended the sheep. His obedience in keeping sheep is what led to him becoming king. It wasn't knowing the right people or being in the right place at the right time, it was his righteous servant's heart (Acts 13:22). When David was appointed king of Israel, Samuel reminded him of the importance his care, devotion, and obedience played in the grand scheme of God's plan: "In times past, when Saul was king over us, it was you who led out and brought in Israel. And the LORD said to you, 'You shall be shepherd of my people Israel, and you shall be prince over Israel'" (2 Sam. 5:2 ESV). David could have believed the lie that he wasn't enough because of what others said and did. But he trusted the process, remained faithful to God, and invested his time and energy pursuing righteousness over recognition.

The next time we come up against the lie that we are not special, we must remember that we are especially important to God.

Not everyone will see the anointing God has placed on our lives, nor will we always be included in everything we think we should. People may count us out because of their own limited view or personal ideas. We can believe we have to be at this event or this stage in our life at a pace that matches our ideal timeline. But both people's validation and our desires are flawed because we are human. We clearly see in this story that God's thoughts, plans, and opinions are higher than our own.

We must trust that God has not forgotten us and He has good things in store for us. Even the greatest gratification this world can bring is short-lived compared to the glory and approval of God. The next time we come up against the lie that we are not special, we must remember that we are especially important to God.

> But you are a *chosen* people, a royal priesthood, a holy nation, *God's special possession*, that you may declare the praises of him who called you out of darkness into his wonderful light. (1 Pet. 2:9, emphasis added)

Lie #2: You Are Not Able

David's courage especially stood out from his elder brothers in one particular story—David versus Goliath. When some of David's elder brothers were soldiers in King Saul's army, they were in a losing battle against the Philistines and their secret weapon—a seven-foot giant named Goliath. Jesse sent David to the battlefield with food for his brothers so they could regain their strength, but when David arrived he found the men trembling at the sight of the giant. It's important to note that while a seven-foot man would seem tall to us today, he was in fact a giant to the soldiers in David's time, who were five feet tall on average. When no one would face the giant, David bravely declared he would go, only to be mocked and dismissed by the soldiers around him. No one believed he was able, including Saul. "Saul replied, 'You are not able to go out against this Philistine and fight him; you are only a young man, and he has been a warrior from his youth'" (1 Sam. 17:33).

Many of us have grand dreams to influence the world, overcome a personal trial, or commit ourselves to a journey of betterment. But the moment one, two, or ten voices tell us we are not able, we succumb to the lie and our courage dies with our dreams and goals.

Saul couldn't see that God doesn't call the equipped, He equips the called. David knew he could defeat Goliath because the Lord was with him, just as He always had been.

> But David said to Saul, "Your servant has been keeping his father's sheep. When a lion or a bear came and carried off a sheep from the flock, I went after it, struck it and rescued the sheep from its mouth. . . . The LORD who rescued me from the paw of the lion and the paw of the bear will rescue me from the hand of this Philistine." (1 Sam. 17:34–35, 37)

The Bible assures us that just as He was with David, God is always with us, making us able to conquer whatever giants we face. I love these verses from the Psalms that remind us all of God's presence and help:

> I lift up my eyes to the hills.
>   From where does my help come?
> My help comes from the LORD,
>   who made heaven and earth.
>
> He will not let your foot be moved;
>   he who keeps you will not slumber. (121:1–3 ESV)

When we face a mountain, our strength must resound from within. We must be like Zerubbabel and shout, "Grace, grace" to see the mountain come crumbling down (Zech. 4:7 ESV). We will have shortcomings because we are human. But it is through grace that we trust that our authority is not in our ability but in our partnership with God. Often the first victory is what we need to step into our authority.

> When the Philistines saw that their hero was dead, they turned and ran. (1 Sam. 17:51)

I'm ready to see our partnership with Christ cause nations to turn from the ways of the world. I'm ready to see our confidence in Christ lead us to do mighty things for Him that cause others to run to Christ. If God can use a young shepherd boy to defeat an entire army, He can use us. When we set out to slay giants, the overpowering lies that have caused us to tremble, we remember Who makes us able.

> As soon as David returned from killing the Philistine, Abner took him and brought him before Saul, with David still holding the Philistine's head. "Whose son are you, young man?" Saul asked him. David said, "I am the son of your servant Jesse of Bethlehem." (vv. 57–58)

We are the daughters of God. On our own we are not able, but through grace, partnership, and heavenly authority, **we are able.**

Lie #3: You Are Not Lovable

It's hard to imagine David—a faithful shepherd, mighty warrior, and victorious king, the man after God's own heart—as being unlovable. But later in life, he was.

In a complicated and extensive feud fit for reality TV, King David's family began to unravel. It started when his son Amnon sexually abused his half-sister Tamar, causing her brother Absalom to want blood that David would not shed. So Absalom took matters into his own hands. After the deed was done, Absalom fled the kingdom for three years. Though he was displeased with Absalom's actions, David missed his son deeply and invited Absalom to return home. But during those years in solitude, Absalom's resentment toward his father ran deep and he decided David was no longer fit to rule. But who should replace him? Who but the young prince himself! Cunningly, he drew supporters to aid his gradual revolt. Like I told you . . . drama, drama, drama.

David became despised by his own son and by effect, his own kingdom. When David heard the news that Absalom had gathered his army and was leading a rebellion, his fight-or-flight response kicked in and he fled the kingdom before his son could attack.

> A messenger came and told David, "The hearts of the people of Israel are with Absalom." Then David said to all his officials who were with him in Jerusalem, "Come! We must flee, or none of us will escape from Absalom. We must leave immediately, or he will move quickly to overtake us and bring ruin on us and put the city to the sword." (2 Sam. 15:13–14)

After days of being on the run, the time came for the two groups to face each other in battle. In my opinion, at this point of desperation, David faced the reality that he couldn't keep running; he had to fight his internal and external battles. When he had to tap back into his fighter muscle memory, he remembered who he was—a man after God's own heart, not man's. While Absalom was seeking revenge and political accession, David was ready to fight for his kingdom and family. David walked in his true strength when he remembered he was loved and chosen by God, and it was from that place that he was able to love and protect others.

> David mustered the men who were with him and appointed over them commanders of thousands and commanders of hundreds. David sent out his troops, a third under the command of Joab, a third under Joab's brother Abishai son of Zeruiah, and a third under Ittai the Gittite. The king told the troops, "I myself will surely march out with you."

> But the men said, "You must not go out; if we are forced to flee, they won't care about us. Even if half of us die, they won't care; but you are worth ten thousand of us. It would be better now for you to give us support from the city." (2 Sam. 18:1–3)

Eventually David's army won the battle, and when trying to flee, Absalom was killed. After the victory, David mourned the loss of his son and made an order to restore peace in the kingdom among all parties.

Thankfully, many of our stories aren't as complicated and deadly as this, but maybe they are as loveless. I don't know who has purposely or unknowingly communicated that you are not loved. Maybe a friend, an ex, a leader, or even you yourself, but you cannot live under that lie. You need to take inventory of the voices you allow to speak into your destiny.

Believing that you are not loved or worthy of love can make you shrink back from who you are called to be. For years I operated from the place of believing I was unlovable. It caused me to settle for less than I was called to and to act out of character, and if I had continued living under that lie, I wouldn't be writing this to you now.

Your decisions can lead you far from God, but nothing can ever make Him love you less. Don't let this be a cliché. Jesus bore all your sins, insecurities, shame, and fears on the cross because of the Father's boundless love for you. I believe God will surround you with people who love you deeply; but even when earthly love fails, God's love won't.

I hope that through David's life you're able to recognize different "are not" lies and call out the ones you've believed. Though seemingly positive, some of the "you are" lies you face are secretly detrimental to your identity. Remember what God says over you: You are special. You are able. You are loved.

Half-Truths: "You Are" Statements

I try to live under the notion that what you see is what you get. I appreciate depth in my relationships; I despise inauthenticity. Meeting someone and realizing I didn't actually meet *them* makes me feel like a fool. There's a reason people are averse to con artists and clowns—they present a facade. We don't enjoy deception. After all, a wolf in sheep's clothing is a predator using innocence to disguise his scheme. This is one reason I believe half-truths can be more devastating and manipulative than complete lies.

A complete lie disregards the truth altogether, but a half-truth puts a dirty little spin on honesty. Did you ever have that one rebellious friend or sibling whose fake alibis would involve you? Say they were throwing a ball in the house and broke something, or they went to the cute senior's party instead of to the library like they'd said. When caught in their deception, they would say something like, "I didn't break it. I was outside with [your name]" or "No, I didn't go to that party. [Your name] and I have been studying for our final exam!" How frustrating to have your truth caught up in their lie.

The devil is a liar; this much we know. It should be no surprise then that the devil also operates in half-truths to hurt creation. His first act on earth was one of deception. Second Corinthians confirms this: "No wonder, for even Satan disguises himself as an angel of light" (11:14 ESV). He doesn't come to us as blatant evil; he comes disguised as good to deceive us about which way is right or wrong. We're all right in our own mind because we operate from a place of love or base our stance on some strand of holy principle. But sometimes we fail to see the twist in the tongue, the fable in the fine print.

See, the devil doesn't care if we pray every day or haven't prayed a day in our life—all he wants is to keep us off the path of righteousness. We must remember that he once was God's right-hand angel, and he knows well the ways of heaven. He knows that the Word of God is the only firm instruction to walking in fullness, so he uses it to his advantage. In the wilderness, the devil didn't rally his myriad of fallen angels to attack Jesus with brute force; he used the spoken Word of God! He took pieces of Scripture and ever so slightly twisted them to try to trick Jesus into sinning against His Father.

I want to dissect the "you are" lies the devil told Adam and Eve long ago in the garden of Eden. In the garden, God gave Adam and Eve specific instructions to freely eat from any tree except the tree of the knowledge of good and evil. They had free choice of any tree and its fruit but were told to stay away from one particular tree because it would bring death. While living under God's instruction, they were content, fed, and satisfied—until they listened to and believed the enemy's lies. The devil saw an opportunity to twist God's words of care and caution to make Him out to be a controlling dictator. The enemy disguised himself as a snake and told Eve three half-truths that changed the dynamic of humanity forever.

> But the serpent said to the woman, "You will not surely die. For God knows that when you eat of it your eyes will be opened, and you will be like God, knowing good and evil." (Gen. 3:4–5 ESV)

Lie #1: You Are above Consequences

Everything Satan said was true, partially. When he said, "You will not surely die," he was right that Adam and Eve would not die immediately in the flesh. But he didn't mention the deadliness of sin that would enter the world. With a partial truth, he deceived them into believing that God's warnings didn't affect them.

He uses that same mentality today, except his disguises have evolved. These disguises vary—media, desires, good intentions, emotions—anything he can use to twist the areas where we don't wholeheartedly know the truth. If we spent five minutes watching the news or scrolling through social media, we would see the same ploy. He exercises half-truths and partial lies to appeal to our senses and impulses and lead us off course. "Sex won't harm you; it will make you feel good!" "Abortion doesn't rob you of the blessing of children; it allows you to exercise more freedom now!" He's sneaky in his delivery. Perhaps that's why his very first deception came through a snake.

If we take the bait, we unknowingly sacrifice the long-term version of desire or freedom for a temporary version with unforeseen pain attached. Adam and Eve wanted to live a full life, but they believed the lie that it could be found by following their own will. That's why we must have a relationship with Jesus and truly know the Word—so we are not deceived.

Lie #2: You Are Missing Out

The serpent made Adam and Eve believe God was withholding something from them. By saying "Your eyes will be opened, and you will be like God, knowing good and evil," he left out the key point that knowing good and evil meant they were now able to experience both. In the garden, they knew nothing but good; they didn't have to decipher between the two for themselves because they knew no evil. The enemy took what God had protected them from and made it seem like He was withholding something from them and keeping it for Himself. He twisted the truth to alter their view of God from a good and giving Father to a greedy and vengeful imposter.

I want to unpack this more here: if we don't believe God is a good Father with good things in store for us, then we will never be able to accept the good things He has waiting for us. If you thought your parents had only bad intentions for your life, you wouldn't listen to them at all. You'd disregard their guidance, wisdom, and input while running in the opposite direction from anything they said. The same is true for God. If you think He wants to take things away from you, to keep the joy and fun for Himself as you remain unfulfilled, you will run to the very things He is trying to protect you from.

The part of this point that terrifies me is that Adam and Eve were in the garden and walked alongside God yet still had room in their hearts for disbelief. We can do everything "right" in our walk with God, but if we're not in an honest relationship with Him, then there's no point. The intimacy we find with God gives us trust to believe Him, vulnerability to work things out with Him, and strength to overcome any temptation.

Lie #3: You Are the Master of Your Life

Our enemy wants us to live in the least powerful state possible. That's why variations of his lies have undertones that many would say are empowering but in reality strip us of power. In the garden, the serpent communicated to Adam and Eve that they could have God status. Because he knows the universal truth that our power, fulfillment, and completion rest in the being of God, he wants to strip that line of power by telling us, "You are the master of your life."

We hear this communicated in subtle ways: "Do whatever feels right to you." "Live your own life." "Be whoever you want to be." "You're born this way." "You know what's best for you." These types of thoughts come from the final lie: "You will be like God." Here the devil suggested that if Adam and Eve rebelled against what God had spoken, then they would be elevated to His status. They exchanged closeness with God for a shot at being equals with Him. Why? Because then they could do whatever they wanted and make the rules up as they went! Sounds like complete freedom, right? Well, not quite. The power to do whatever we want whenever we want comes with a weight no man or woman should ever have to bear. Walking under God's instruction allows us to live in joy and peace while being completely free from burden or guilt.

God was meant to be the commander in chief of our lives; He knows the map of eternity like the back of His hand. He can see everything—all the traps, the right routes, and the wrong ones. Adam and Eve had the perfect guide but kicked Him to the curb just so they could be the ones in the driver's seat.

Imagine you're taking a road trip with a friend who has GPS and you don't. They're driving and the trip is going well. You get to sit back with your feet up, enjoying whatever candy you got from the last gas station. (I hope you picked Sour Patch Kids or Snickers.) But halfway through the trip, you decide you could do a better job. It's not that your friend did anything to make you doubt their ability to get you to the right destination—you just want to be in control.

Your friend hears you out and pulls over to let you try your hand behind the wheel. As the tires hit the pavement, you're feeling confident. *See, there's nothing to it*, you think. You start to drive down unfriendly paths, with no way to tell if you're heading the right way. You don't panic but keep your composure, because you wouldn't dare let your friend see that you might not know what you're doing. A few hours pass, and as you begin to admit to yourself that you could be lost, your eyes get heavy and your stomach aches. *It sure would be easier if I were still in the passenger seat*, you think.

Unfortunately, many of us don't pull over. Call it pride, fear, determination, or whatever, we keep driving. I worry many of us have been lied to without knowing it, all because we were in the driver's seat. No matter who you are, you need a guide, a helper, a friend. What makes the lost found, the weary strong, and the exhausted restful is all the same answer—pulling over and letting Jesus back in the driver's seat.

The enemy's tactic of tainting the truth—be it his "you are not" or "you are" shams, his whole lies or half-truths—isn't a mere distraction. It's an attack we should take seriously! Some of the most menacing commanders in history were deceptively mesmerizing. Adolf Hitler, Saddam Hussein, and Osama bin Laden all rallied armies through their cunning speeches, political persuasion, and radical ability to frame what was morally wrong as ethically right. If mere men can pose such a threat, we shouldn't doubt our enemy can do the same and more. Our enemy is damned, but he isn't dumb—he was able to deceive a third of the angels to follow him in his rebellion. But taking his threat seriously doesn't mean we need to fear it; we just need to be aware and prepared.

This is a battle. We can learn more about an appropriate warfare response from Sun Tzu. The general writes, "If you know the enemy and know yourself, you need not fear the result of a hundred battles. If you know yourself but not the enemy, for every victory gained you will also suffer a defeat. If you know neither the enemy nor yourself, you will succumb in every battle."[2]

The enemy's weapons of choice and battle plans are exposed. The only piece left to ensure our victory is to know ourselves. Do you? Today the idea seems to be ever-changing based on what season of life you're in or what societal teachings you're under at the time. There's only one avenue to discovering ourselves. When we reach that point—victory.

Our relationship with Christ is crucial to breaking *every* stronghold in our lives. The world operates under its own skewed belief system, and the only way to combat these lies is to live by the truth. Society tells us that our worth is found in superficial areas. Yet putting our identity, hope, or comfort in these things leaves us susceptible to the snakes lurking behind each corner.

Until we know the Truth (Christ), we will keep falling for half-truths.

We will never find fullness until we know what it looks like. We will never know how to have healthy marriages until we know what they look like. We will never satisfy that burning desire of purpose until we know what makes life purposeful. Until we know the Truth (Christ), we will keep falling for half-truths.

Knowing Truth comes by mirroring, a powerful tool I learned from journalism. This is when we mimic the body language, demeanor, or vocal pitch of someone we're speaking with. Research reports this tactic can be highly rewarding. When mirroring was used correctly, waitresses gained higher tips, women found more success in speed dating, and salesclerks closed more deals.[3] Pretty nifty trick, huh?

But there's a caveat—we can't just mirror anyone at any time. That's because mirroring is not an action but a reaction. It's usually done subconsciously; our body follows our brain. As our mind is interested in what someone is saying verbally, our body becomes interested in what they're doing nonverbally. While it's a powerful tool to draw us in and get the most from our counterpart, the skill is successful only when we are genuinely engaged and interested in what our counterpart is saying or doing.

In the same way we can't mirror someone we're inattentive or indifferent to, we can't mirror God by shallowly connecting to Him or surface-skimming His Word. Memorizing what the Word says isn't much help if we're not making time to know Who the Word is. On a date, we can tell the difference between a guy who knows all the right things to say and a guy who is genuinely interested in us. Regarding God, our interest and attention must be genuine, and we must deeply trust Him and where He leads.

When we are in relationship with Him, we become more like Him. Because His Word is truth, by knowing Him, we know the Truth. Truly knowing ourselves is to understand the intricate creation God called us to be, and that creation is made in His image.

Have you ever wondered why many new Christians explain that believing in Jesus makes them feel like themselves for the very first time? It's because we are wired to God. Deep calls to deep. There will be a cavernous longing left unfilled until we are united with Christ. We will not fully satisfy that longing until we're with Him in eternity, but it begins here on earth as our spirits are in relationship with His Spirit.

08. Help My Unbelief

Faith is the bird that feels the light when the dawn is still dark.

—Rabindranath Tagore

We did it! Hallelujah!

We made it through the chaotic years of the COVID-19 pandemic! What a time. All the world was connected as we faced the same threat. For a short while the world stopped, each country focused on how to handle the pandemic.

Many practices worked and many didn't. Much was trial and error. Here in America, many buildings and businesses were shut down, deemed nonessential. We wondered, *How does one define what is and isn't essential?*

Agriculture, pharmacy, banking, gas, and lodging were a few deemed essential. I'm thankful I wasn't the person in charge of giving business owners the green or red light. It'd simply be too difficult to filter through which companies and corporations were vital or important.

When it comes to our lives, however, we already have a framework to know what practices and principles are essential to how we think and live. No matter what line of business we're in, or where we live, we share the same key essential need—faith.

What is faith? It's our oxygen—everything else is dependent on it. Nothing else can operate without it. It's our footing—we don't get far or stand strong without it. Jesus says in John 5:24, "Truly, truly, I say to you, whoever hears my word and believes him who sent me has eternal life" (ESV).

Faith is our fundamental essence and our first defense. It guards our lives and our hearts. This is a great stopping point for you to ask yourself, "In what have I placed my faith?" Maybe you believe in God or go to church, but when you probe inside, your faith isn't at the place you'd like it to be. Or you long to trust God, but there's so much messiness in between where you are and where He seems to be.

In this chapter, we'll dive into why faith is essential and how our faith can dwindle or tap out. Because it is essential, I want you to be equipped—not caught in a trap that slowly robs your "faith bank" without you noticing. If Jesus chided the disciples for being those "of little faith" (Matt. 8:26) even as they walked with Him, then it's not such a bad idea for you and me to make sure our faith levels are high.

Faith in the Waiting

I detest going to the DMV.

Maybe it's the combination of feeling lost as soon as you walk in and being subjected to a queue process you have no say in. Every line and room look the same. Is this the one for driver's license or tag renewal? I don't have to explain the process in length because you know the drill—take a number and wait in line. That's always the worst part—waiting. It seems endless. *Tick, tock. Tick, tock.* Minutes feel like hours. Where is a Disney FastPass when you really need it?

When we moved to Tennessee, we went five times within less than a year just to register our one vehicle. FIVE TIMES! Each time, there was something wrong with the paperwork from the out-of-state dealership we had bought the car from, and we had to start the cycle all over again. On my final visit to the DMV, at nine months pregnant and after standing in line for over an hour, they had to unlock the door just to let me out—everyone else who had been waiting had already gotten their tags and gone home. But the important thing when I walked out that day was that I had what I came for. Though it was extensive and tiresome, my waiting had not been in vain.

Sometimes faith comes with waiting or delay. But don't let the delay give way to doubt.

Sarah was skeptical too. She even laughed before the Lord at the thought that after her childbearing years had passed, she'd finally bear a child (Gen. 18). And while Sarah laughed at her barrenness, Hannah wept over hers (1 Sam. 1). She wept to the point that the priest Eli thought she was drunk in the middle of the day, as she exclaimed, "I'm a woman brokenhearted" (v. 15 MSG). While Hannah wept as she waited to start her family, Joseph wept as he waited to be reunited with his (Gen. 45). He waited so long that his family didn't recognize him when they first saw him.

We're used to the instantaneous. Not knowing makes us a nervous wreck as we wait. Delays can give way to doubt as question after question arises: "When is it going to be my turn?" "Why do I have to wait?" "Has God forgotten me?"

> Sometimes faith comes with waiting or delay. But don't let the delay give way to doubt.

There was a video that came across my feed just this morning. In it, TV show host Steve Harvey shared a reassuring anecdote. He said, "When you ask God for something, God boxes it up, puts your name on it and He ships it the day you ask for it. . . . The problem with the package is He never tells you the date that it's going to arrive. If He did that, it would destroy the one element that He requires—your faith."[1] I'm not sure what packages you or Steve Harvey have been praying for, but I know this is true: if we need all the answers, we're relying on control, not faith. The questions, waiting, and trust all build our reliance on Him.

More telling than any tracking number are the number of times God has proven Himself faithful.

In any relationship, you expect the other person to be faithful. On your wedding day, you exchange vows—personal promises for your marriage. They often revolve around a dedication to love that person with all your heart, declaring you'll always be faithful and keep their best interests at heart. It's a romantic proclamation for a husband and wife to declare their love in front of their friends and family. But how romantic or trusting would it have been if, on my wedding day, I recited vows so loving that Shakespeare wished he'd written them himself, only to follow with this contingency: "And I vow all this *if* you sign a prenup."

No, I don't have a secret stash of millions or an offshore account that I need to protect, but for some of us, just putting our hearts on the line is too risky without some backup compensation. "What if I trust in God's plan and it doesn't work out?" If you look at Scripture, you'll see God rarely assured anyone that everything would go easy peasy lemon squeezy. But He did give us some promises that steady us in the waiting and put our doubts to rest:

He will be with you always (Matt. 28:20).
His love for you will never run out (1 Chron. 16:34).
His plans for you are good (Jer. 29:11).

When we find our faith wavering, we can rest assured that God was, is, and will continue to be faithful. Mark 9 is one of the truest testaments to the inner tension believers go through in keeping faith when faced with doubt. Verses 14–29 tell the story of a worried father who asked Jesus to heal his possessed son. He was amid disciples and religious leaders asking frantically for someone to drive out the demon harming his son. The disciples tried and failed. The religious leaders watched and argued. It was a hot mess of frantic pleas and frustrated priests when Jesus finally came onto the scene.

I love that Jesus tended to withdraw from crowds and appear at gatherings "fashionably late." His tendency to delay wasn't due to a lack of punctuality. Christ would wait until the stage had been set for the miracle at hand. His timing was always intentional.

The father was surely swimming in uncertainty about why his son wasn't being healed and if he ever would be. He was probably tired of hearing, despite his efforts, that he couldn't get what he sought. He'd asked and asked, without any sign of healing coming. He could have exhausted his faith, he could have hopped back on his horse or donkey and said, "Forget this!" But he stayed—waiting on a miracle—until Jesus came.

Two things were surely rumbling in his mind: what he'd seen and what he'd believed. He'd believed this rabbi and His disciples could heal his son, but he still stood there empty-handed. As he was explaining his son's condition and crying out for Jesus to save him, he murmured a statement that is caught somewhere between belief and skepticism: "But if you can do anything, take pity on us and help us" (v. 22). There was an ask and an apprehension. Jesus immediately addressed the soft spots in this father's request and gently poked at them, asking, "'*If* you can?' . . . Everything is possible for one who believes" (v. 23, emphasis added). Without making excuses, without becoming offended, without ridiculing others in the equation, the father replied, "I do believe; help me overcome my unbelief!" (v. 24).

If this were a marital relationship, this father was essentially standing at the altar saying, "I do, but . . ." "But I'm still waiting." "But I feel helpless." "But I'm scared." He had cold feet, but he didn't run off. He was involved enough to be honest about his level of faith. He desired to be connected to God and to trust Him, but he battled fear and doubt. I like this. How easily he could have shrugged and turned away in embarrassment or defeat. He could have spat at His feet and angrily demanded of Jesus, "Do it now or else, you rabbi!" But he didn't; he admitted his lack of faith and asked for help where his soul was weak. I like this example because it's not only humbling but also helpful. We can do only so much on our own. Even in your faith journey, you will realize at times that you need an extra measure of His Holy Spirit for instruction, direction, and understanding.

Be comfortable enough with God to come to Him when you sense doubt or disbelief rising within. When you need an extra measure, His love flows measureless. Your miracle may not come in the same manner or at the same time as someone else's. It may not come in the packaging or on the estimated date you expected. Keep the faith in the waiting.

God's not intimidated by what we come up against that has the potential to sway our thoughts. He's not put off when we must rally around what we know to be true and ask Him questions. We hurt only ourselves when we turn away from Him and remain in our own doubt.

If you find yourself questioning God's goodness or if you are on the right path—go to Him. The honesty we find in admitting where we are struggling only strengthens our relationship with our Father. He is more than gracious to process with us, give us peace that surpasses all understanding, and bring certainty to any chaos.

Maybe like this father in Mark 9, you're waiting on a miracle. You may be questioning, "Is it even possible?" or "Jesus, are you really there?" The questions doubt digs up can either cause us to drift from God or go deeper in faith. Some of the best things of God can't yet be seen in the natural (eternity, His Spirit, etc.). Everything we're connected to in the natural is palpable, but God is a wind unconfined—what our eyes cannot see and our hands cannot grasp must be nurtured and held within our hearts.

The wind blows where it wishes, and you hear its sound, but you do not know where it comes from or where it goes. So it is with everyone who is born of the Spirit. (John 3:8 ESV)

The waiting can show what's out of order or missing, like my waiting game at the DMV. Maybe there's something you still need. A piece of the puzzle, a lesson to be learned, a chapter to be closed. When the father and the disciples didn't see the outcome they'd expected, they didn't turn away; they turned to Jesus to ask for guidance. There are lessons He teaches us as we wait on Him. Perhaps the waiting is not about the amount of time we spend in line but about the lessons we learn and what's produced in us while we wait.

Sarah learned never to doubt God's promises and produced an heir for God's promise of the coming Messiah.

Hannah learned never to compare someone else's timeline to her own and produced powerful prayers amid personal pain.

Joseph learned that God's blessings can come from unexpected paths and produce an abundance of good for those who treated him badly.

We want to measure the waiting by time, but our God, who is neither limited nor defined by time, measures waiting by faith. His faithfulness is not dependent on His promises coming quickly or slowly. It's like the thrilling movie your friend begs you to watch, pleading, "Just wait until the ending!" Your miracle is not lost in the mail. Your faith is not broken. It's not over until the faithful One says so. God's Word is always the final word.

> The LORD is good to those who wait for him,
> to the soul who seeks him. (Lam. 3:25 ESV)

Having faith in the waiting is essentially having faith that God's plan is worth the wait. The next time you feel impatient or fretful while waiting, bring this verse to mind. His nature is good, His blessings are good, and yes, His timing is good too. Wearing the Word like a banner keeps our thoughts and emotions in line with His instruction. Like a friendly voice gently reminding us, "Don't wander too far ahead" or "Don't worry, dear," it keeps us steady when the waves of our feelings are strong enough to capsize our well-being. Faith can outlast and outwork what surges from waiting and worry.

Faith in the Midst of Fear

Sometimes I think we need one of those "No Soliciting" signs for some of the advice we receive. Especially during pregnancy.

When I was growing up, nearly everyone around me described childbirth as the worst pain of their life or the burden we bear thanks to Eve's sin. Yikes, not the jolliest pep talk! I thought surely when the time came for me to give birth, I'd gladly take any medicine the doctors offered me. I'm a petite woman, after all. There's not much room for that pain to spread throughout my 5'5" body. A medicated hospital delivery would have been a perfectly acceptable birth plan. But what, or who, was leading me to that decision? Was it out of comfort, concern, or others' comments?

Immediately after I learned I was pregnant with my first child, I began praying over him and for God's hand to be evident throughout those nine months we were both growing. One day when I was praying, probably rebuking morning sickness, I felt God say, *You're going to have a natural delivery.*

"Nope. No way. God, I think you've got your wires crossed today. I can't do that."

He prompted back, *Why not?*

Then it hit me.

In that moment, I realized I'd been thrilled to become a mother but terrified of delivering the baby. It wasn't solely due to the horror stories I'd heard or the horrible scenes movies depicted; it was personal. I'd had brokenness spoken over my pregnancy far before we ever began trying to start a family. I recounted the very phrases that I'd let build my faith in fear: "You won't do well pregnant." "You don't do good with pain." "You're going to struggle navigating all the pregnancy symptoms."

Before I was an expectant mother, I only considered pregnancy through the lens of fear—what could go wrong and how it would negatively affect me. Every decision I made stemmed from the belief that what those women had said was accurate. I had so much faith in their words and so little faith in myself.

As Arden and I began our first doctor's appointment, our expecting-parents glow quickly escaped us. The doctor met our smiles with a scowl. I'm not sure what exactly I'd expected, but I figured there would be some congratulations or helpful information to commemorate this trajectory we were setting out on. When we began the ultrasound, at first the experience was surreal—it was *my* belly getting the warm gel because we were going to see *our* baby!

As the sonographer scanned my still-small belly, she was silent. She began the next test and remained silent. "Hmm, that could be the embryo there, but it's pretty small. Why don't you let us know if you have any bleeding this week."

Bleeding was not the *B* word I'd expected to come out of her mouth. I wanted to shout, "There *is* a *baby* growing, and he/she is perfectly healthy!" But I didn't . . . not because I'm controlled and composed in difficult circumstances but because that fear that had begun clouding my pregnancy long ago was doing its dark deeds now. I began thinking, *What if I'm not pregnant—or worse, I am but I'm losing my baby?*

You're going to struggle being pregnant, remember?

All those symptoms you're going to have . . . here they begin.

I left that office defeated. This was a defining moment. I had to ask myself, "Are you going to grow in fear or grow in faith?" The answer was easy; the application not so much. Choosing faith meant leaning into the apprehension of the unknown and going out on a limb instead of down the road of least resistance, which we're much more familiar and comfortable with. What is familiar and comfortable to you?

Pregnancy was already a new journey for me. Most of the moms I knew had chosen different routes. I wasn't sure what I was signing up for, but in choosing faith, I knew I was cosigning with God. Come what may, His Word promised He would be by my side.

My faith in what He was calling me to was even smaller than my two-month-old developing baby, but just like this child, I knew it would grow in time.

I wanted to meet every facet of welcoming my child into the world with the faith that God had created me for this assignment! Your approach may be different from mine; what's important is that as mamas, we lead with faith and believe God is with us through the entire process, and His perfect love casts out fear.

I faced the rest of my pregnancy with a natural-minded approach. We switched to a birthing center, made a natural and nutrient-dense food plan, and watched as God led us through each month and decision along the way, meeting every milestone with increasing provision. My baby and I were healthy and thriving. A tangible grace accompanied my yes. Everything within my pregnancy journey followed a beautiful, faithful rhythm.

As His grace brushed my faith, I felt the enemy wasn't too happy about it. This fear mentality had been a long project he'd been working on within me; in a swift move, God took the lead. As we progressed through the months, I didn't struggle with pregnancy symptoms, but I did have a few struggles to overcome. I didn't have horrible hormones, but I did have a car wreck. A few weeks later, I caught a wave of food poisoning that made me and my bathroom close friends. A few weeks later—*BAM!*—another bout of food poisoning. This time it took my appetite completely. And then a few days later, I got food poisoning *again*. This time it was E. coli, and I was afraid not for myself but for our baby.

My mama heart was overwhelmed, and I began having signs of a panic attack—something I hadn't experienced in years. Arden wrapped his arms around me and spoke faith over our child. "Thank you, Lord, that he is healthy and whole and that You are his ultimate Provider!" As I prayed with him, I stopped shaking; the fear that was creeping back in was shoved away as my faith rose to another level. I had been praying for God to care for me so I could care for our child, but that day I realized He was providing not only for me but also for our son. Everything we'd needed, He had supplied. It wasn't all on me; God carried us both.

And as the verse goes, we do not have to fear, for He strengthens and upholds us (Ps. 89:21). Though we face fear-enticing circumstances, it's in those moments when our faith and fear battle it out. As we step into this sort of spiritual arena, we can look to those before us who also experienced the same thing. Joshua was nervous, dare I say even anxious, to step into his predecessor's role of conquering the promised land. It was a lofty task and risky business. But God encouraged and even commanded Joshua to put courage over fear, for He'd be with him wherever he went (Josh. 1:1–9). Paul, who encountered numerous fear-invoking circumstances himself—from being shipwrecked and bitten by a venomous snake to facing the demented, anti-Christian King Nero—could speak from personal experience on the topic of choosing faith over fear. In his epistle to the Romans, he reminds readers that our anxieties are no match for our God (Rom. 8:31).

Though we face battles in this life, when we put our faith in Him, we find the power to rebuke strongholds and conquer struggles.

I've seen, at least in my life, that God's instruction is often twofold. He showed me that my faith yielded the power to replace the lies with blessings. Though we face battles in this life, when we put our faith in Him, we find the power to rebuke strongholds *and* conquer struggles. Our faith is both our catalyst and our support; it moves us through this life, keeping our hearts on God. Some believe that if a situation causes pain or is trying for us, then we just don't have faith. Well, from the stories throughout the Bible, we see this isn't the case.

Jesus made sure His disciples experienced the fullness of faith and saw miracles up close. Some days, faith lessons were miraculous, providing sustenance from fish and bread for thousands. Other days faith lessons involved Jesus sleeping through a storm while the disciples had to sweat it out and decide how to respond. We need both experiences. Only God knows which one we need in each moment. Because He wants you and me to be discipled, He doesn't spare us from one or the other. Sometimes our faith will look like receiving a random check just before rent is due, and other times it will be holding on to Him as we receive a devastating diagnosis. Hebrews 11:1 proclaims, "Now faith is confidence in what we hope for and assurance about what we do not see."

The more we understand this verse, the more we will better utilize our faith and trust God's working through every day, every event. I had a handful of affirmations I kept by my bedside in my third trimester, but I wish this verse had been one of them. I had heard so many stories of women's supernatural and pain-free births, I began to believe the only way to experience God's faithfulness in the delivery room was if He delivered me from any and all pain.

Faith in the Midst of Pain

We often interpret Ephesians 3:20–21 as straightforward verses about faith:

> Now to him who is able to do immeasurably more than all we ask or imagine, according to his power that is at work within us, to him be glory.

The presumed equation is that if we put our faith in God, we get a lavish reward. Bigger houses and better spouses, bigger checks and blinged-out necks. It's true, His blessings can bring increase and benefit, but that doesn't mean they're always wrapped in a bow. Like all Scripture, we must read these verses through the lens by which they were written and intended.

When we decipher these verses with the context of our reality here on earth plus our limited vantage point, we can see that there's more to it. Romans 8:28 says God always works things together for His good—but what if His good is not always what looks good? At least in the moment.

Paul wrote Ephesians in shackles, literal chains. Yet these verses were written as a doxology, an expression of praise for God. When he was lowly, when he could have deemed God unfaithful, Paul chose to praise Him and encourage others to put their hope in Him.

When in Rome, do as the apostles do! That's the saying, right?

Arden and I were able to visit *Carcere Mamertino*, Mamertine Prison, when we visited Rome. It's believed to be the prison where Paul wrote the epistles and spent his final days. Unlike American prisons, which are built on level ground and offer skill-building classes and outdoor recreation, this prison was primitive—a dungeon levels belowground without windows, bathrooms, or sufficient space to move or stand. Prisoners suffered in these conditions. But the great mystery of faith is that through this trial, Paul remained faithful. He writes,

In him and through faith in him we may approach God with freedom and confidence. I ask you, therefore, not to be discouraged because of my sufferings for you, which are your glory. (Eph. 3:12–13)

There's a tension-filled juxtaposition, especially in American Christianity, that God works through either prosperity or suffering. You've probably heard exclamations about both. The tie to prosperity pulls from James 4:2, while the tie to suffering pulls from Matthew 6:24. Both these thoughts camp out in one lane, putting their faith in one result. Prosperous expectancy entrusts that in His goodness, God gives us abundantly. Sufferance concludes that the only true need we have in this life is Christ.

Both are true.

The coexistence of these two is the essence of faith. It's both/and, not either/or. By faith we obtain and by faith we sustain. I never saw this more clearly than through the experience of giving birth to our firstborn. I wanted a quick, pain-free, I-still-look-camera-ready-postbaby kind of birth with a six-pound babe. I thought that would be a testament of God's kindness and power—that through the abundance of care and covering, I could testify to other women that they could do this! God had given me a few signs to assure me it was time for delivery. From the name of the midwife on call to the type of weather outside, it was so clear He was preparing me for a supernatural birth! But supernatural doesn't mean super easy.

Around 11:00 a.m. on July 25, I went into labor and gave birth at 11:23 a.m. on July 26. Yes, the dates are correct. No typos! My labor was twenty-four hours of the unprecedented and unexpected, with a few whispers from God that gave me the endurance I needed to get through.

The first few hours went so smoothly that Arden had to convince me I was actually in labor. Once my contractions were three minutes apart and one minute long, I accepted that it was time, and we got in the car with smiles on our faces—we were going to meet our baby soon!

Arden, my sister-in-law, Juli, and I arrived at the birth center just before 1:00 a.m., and my midwife welcomed us with worship music playing. I felt calm and ready. Everything was aligning. But the smooth and steady rhythm I'd been in must have fallen out of the car on our way in. Hours passed, contractions continued to quicken and increase, but my cervix wasn't dilating at the same speed. All I could do was wait.

My team took turns throughout the night trying to sleep. I had felt so prepared and expectant, but when the sunlight began peeking through the blinds and I'd barely made any progress, my body wanted to throw in the towel. It started to fight the contractions; the pain grew and I puked over and over again. After a few more hours, I looked at my husband and tearfully exclaimed, "I can't do this. It's not working. We're getting nowhere. Get me out of here!" In that moment, all I wanted was something to make the labor speed up or hurt less. That's when Heather, the midwife from my previous checkup, walked in. She was phenomenal, and she and my team encouraged and challenged me to stick to what I'd prepared for.

At 10:00 a.m. we decided to check my progress again. *Okay, God, we have to be getting close now, surely!* Nope. In ten hours, I had dilated only three centimeters more. I was fading in and out, feeling defeated from assuming I was failing. I wanted an out again, and at this point I pleaded to quit and go to the hospital. This wasn't how it was supposed to be.

It was then that I remembered something a friend did at my baby shower. She clasped my hands in hers and said God was going to be with me, hand in hand, just like our hands were then, throughout my delivery.

Interestingly enough, when we pulled into the birthing center earlier that day, I saw that the sign on the building across the street had an illustration of two hands interlocked. Had God been here holding me this entire time? Was this all His faithfulness packaged differently than I'd imagined? Though I felt overlooked and let down, I chose to cling to what I knew to be true—I was not abandoned. This was where the rubber met the road. It had been easy to believe God was with me throughout my healthy pregnancy, but at the pinnacle of this experience it wasn't so simple. Delivering naturally wasn't coming natural to me. But God didn't promise it would be easy. He promised it would be supernatural.

I clung to God's reminder that our strength accompanies His presence, which is with us always (Deut. 31:6), and felt an internal shift. As my spirit took over, my body worked with the contractions again. Suddenly I felt the urge to push. The midwife suggested we check my dilation first since I was only six centimeters last time we checked. (Remember, you need to be ten centimeters before your baby can pass through the birth canal.) When I moved to the bed, I paused as a wave of maternal instinct swept over me and I exclaimed, "He's coming!" It was a shock to everyone, including me. Seeing his head, the midwife confirmed: it really was time. But almost instantly it retreated. She discovered his upper body was stuck behind my pubic bone in a condition termed shoulder dystocia. My team stepped in to assist, and the nurse rang the alarm for more help. *You will never leave me nor forsake me*, I remembered. For my son's safety, I needed to stay calm, keep pushing, and trust that God was in control. Minutes later, by a miracle, Azariah arrived without injury or other complications.

As Heather placed him on my chest, I looked in disbelief. Twenty-four hours after my labor began, our baby boy arrived at over eight pounds and twenty-one inches long. He was here, he was healthy, and he was absolutely beautiful.

When we reach our breaking point, when we feel broken down, we need God's help—as I did at my lowest. I know it was my faith in Him that carried me. His hand was locked in mine, giving me the strength I needed to the very end. Even when I wanted to throw in the towel, even when I thought I had nothing left, He held me.

> I will strengthen you and help you;
> I will uphold you with my righteous right hand. (Isa. 41:10)

We picked Azariah's name in 2019, long before we knew we were expecting. It means "God helps." And as I reflect on his birth, the definition rings true. God was with us in every detail, and though my birth journey looked different than I'd expected, it was still completely supernatural. God's presence was superabundant. I'll carry a new strength the rest of my life from this process, one I wouldn't have gained without God's guidance and the amazing people in the room with me. I have a new awe for women and the remarkable ability our bodies have to carry and birth children.

Life may not always be comfortable, but pain is temporary. My faith was only prepared for natural delivery if the circumstances were ideal. If I had known all my labor would entail, I would have most likely chosen a different route. I would have told you it was impossible, that I couldn't do it. But maybe that's what the "more" really is in Ephesians 3:20—"Now to him who is able to do immeasurably more than all we ask or imagine"—the impossible.

That's what God does. He doesn't leave us where we've been or where it's always comfortable, because He knows there's more ahead just past our comfort zones. He doesn't give us the full road map because we'd tap out before we even began. When situations feel overwhelming, He gives us more strength. When outcomes look limited, He reveals more than our eyes can see. When our self-deprecation paints an image of inadequacy, He unveils more hidden under the outer layer of our perception.

> With man this is impossible, but with God all things are possible. (Matt. 19:26)

If God moves through the seemingly impossible, then suffering and blessing are both pathways for Him to move in our lives. Now, in no way can I contrast Paul's imprisonment with my labor, but we can combine the attributes of faith—the blessing and the suffering. Through the aching of my birth journey, I came to rely on God in a way I never had to before. Maybe that's why it's called labor? I realized that more than I needed the absence of pain, immediate relief, or an assurance that everything was going to be okay, I needed the guarantee that He was near and His will was being done. It was through enduring the process that He lent His strength. As much as I had hoped for a pain-free birth, if granted, I would have had a strengthless birth. I walked away knowing I'm feeble, but my God is not. And I discovered a strength hidden within me that only deep longing could uncover.

If you've heard only horror stories about motherhood or giving birth, I assure you that it's a beautiful assignment. Or if you're scared to face something different—maybe a new job, a breakup you know is needed, or an area of pain in your life—know that when you face a situation with fear, you act in fear, but when you lead in faith, you act in faith! Like growing a baby, growing in faith comes with stretching, but when you welcome it, you can expect the miraculous!

Exceedingly more isn't always what we expect it to be. Sometimes it's a broken heart, a broken dream, or a broke bank account. But through it all, God is good. We have faith in the promise, not the outcome. If faith is not seeing but believing, it makes sense that we can't foresee what He sees, but we still believe that, despite the fog or confusion, He is good.

Faith in Abundance

Jesus isn't a stranger to fear, or any of our feelings for that matter. Hebrews 4 states that Christ empathizes with what we feel because he experienced these emotions for Himself: "For we do not have a high priest who is unable to sympathize with our weaknesses, but one who in every respect has been tempted as we are, yet without sin" (v. 15 ESV).

Furthermore, Hebrews 5:7–9 says,

> During the days of Jesus' life on earth, he offered up prayers and petitions with fervent cries and tears to the one who could save him from death, and he was heard because of his reverent submission. Son though he was, he learned obedience from what he suffered and, once made perfect, he became the source of eternal salvation for all who obey him.

And through it all, He remained faithful to the end. He was faithful the night before His crucifixion, asking God to take the assignment from Him if God was willing. He was faithful on the cross, experiencing pain you and I can only imagine and trusting that God's plan was good. He was even faithful as a witness to God's mercy in the middle of His suffering, pardoning the thief on His right as he proclaimed his repentance. Today, and forever, He is the faithful One enthroned in heaven, inviting us to also have faith in Him.

This is an invitation we wholeheartedly want to RSVP to. It's the greatest act of love we will see. God gave His Son and the Son gave His life, all so you and I could receive eternal life, unconditional love, and unmatched authority—*if* we so believe. No one can uninvite us or steal our invitation. We're VIPs, and He very much wants us to draw near and stay close to Him.

Fear, timelines, and storms cannot break what's been extended to us. His love is unbreakable. But we must set our faith in God— not in what we control, not in our fears or doubts, not in others, but in God alone.

For I am convinced that neither death nor life, neither angels nor demons, neither the present nor the future, nor any powers, neither height nor depth, nor anything else in all creation, will be able to separate us from the love of God that is in Christ Jesus our Lord. (Rom. 8:38–39)

09. Actually, We Can't Stay Friends

> Everyone thinks of changing the world, but no one thinks of changing himself.
>
> —Leo Tolstoy

After a breakup, have you ever been hit with the oh-so-taboo line "Can we still be friends?"

What a line! If the relationship was particularly long or the breakup was out of the blue, the question could feel less like a sweet remark and more like a slap in the face. If you envisioned yourself potentially marrying this person, then remaining friends, at least close friends, may not be the healthiest situation. For the high school sweethearts and hopeful romantics, some separation is probably needed to calm the sting.

After all, what would that relationship look like? Would Mr. Friend still come around for family gatherings? How awkward would Thanksgiving be if you brought your new boyfriend home to meet your parents, but old boyfriend was also at the dinner table? Your partner would feel like he was eating the crumbs off Mr. Friend's plate. No, no, no; that just wouldn't do!

Or let's say you initiated the separation and broke things off because the relationship had been toxically codependent or unhealthily fueled. That's not a relationship or friendship that would serve you well. Could that ex continue to drunk call you or come over whenever he wanted because you're still "friends"? Uh-uh, that wouldn't do either.

A necessary breakup needs to be a clean break. You can't heal with broken fragments or old tissue still in place. You need a chance to heal *fully*. Often unhealthy breakups are tied to an unhealthy, or less developed, version of you. As you heal, you grow. The old ways of that relationship no longer fit the mold of who you're becoming. As you heal from brokenness, you embrace wholeness. It's time to separate from the old ways that no longer serve you. You don't want to stay friends with an ex, and you don't want to keep old habits around.

Ever wonder why the "new year, new me" model rarely works? Because we're trying to date the new before we break up with the old. We can get a gym membership, but if we're still going to bed with those powdered doughnuts, flaming-hot Doritos, and sour gummy worms (a personal favorite), then our stamina and results in the gym will be different than we were hoping for. I know from personal experience. I've always enjoyed physical exercise. I grew up being active and even played tennis in college, but my love for chocolate was my downfall. My good genes may have helped me look good in jeans, but as soon as I'd put on a bikini there was no hiding the fact that I was "skinny fat."

I finally realized that exercise alone wasn't going to shape my exterior—it was only half the equation for a healthy, fit physique. Once I started eating more nutritious foods and fewer Edwards Chocolate Crème Pies, my health improved and my cravings decreased. I'm embarrassed to say that before I changed my eating habits, I could eat half a pie in one sitting. That creamy, dairy-topped dessert was so good going down but not so good when it started showing down by my derriere. To put it into context, I weighed less leaving the birth center the day I delivered Azariah than I did on my wedding day. What we carry inside matters.

Our new hopes can go only so far while we're entertaining old habits.

Your "new year, new you" goals need more than a Times Square countdown to count in your life—the new you needs space to take root.

Genuinely becoming the new you is achieved by breaking away from the old—old habits, old ways of thinking, old relationships. Hasta la vista, baby! This is the part where you blast some T. Swift— I mean old-school "Teardrops on My Guitar" kind of T. Swift—and shake it off! The final part of breaking up with what broke you is severing your ties to anything associated with your past self. It's time to burn the photos, toss the love notes, and rid your closet of those old sweatshirts. It's time for a **change**.

Open to Change

The word *change* often gets a bad rap because it can imply that if someone is trying to change you, it's because you are unlikable, flawed, or unsuitable. But what if change is less about disapproving of yourself and more about developing yourself? You change a flat tire because the former is no longer suited for the drive. You change your hair because you think your old style no longer suits you.

Think about change in the sense of seasons. Bright summers change to brisk falls; blistering winters change to blooming springs. The cycle of change between each season is never-ending, yet each season brings its own glory. While in each, we embrace it fully with all it brings. But I wonder if we would do the same if the cycle suddenly stopped. If we had only summer, would we wish the heat away? If we had only winter, would we tire of the snow?

The consistent ebb and flow of change is what helps us appreciate the season we are in. I want to apply that same idea to the seasons of life. Every season we go through brings its own glory. But when we abandon the cycle of change, especially when God is calling us to a new season, we devalue what He has set before us. We must open our minds, realizing that change is not the enemy—complacency is. We will never grow in any area unless we fully open ourselves up to the idea that change is essential and necessary.

William James, a philosopher and the first educator to lead a psychology class in America, claimed, "The greatest discovery of our generation is that human beings can alter their lives by altering their attitudes of mind. As you think, so shall you be."[1] What you believe of yourself you will emanate. We see this thought amplified in Proverbs 23:7, "For as he thinketh in his heart, so is he" (KJV).

> We will never grow in any area unless we fully open ourselves up to the idea that change is essential and necessary.

I basically just "poetry punched" you with the idea that growth is 1) necessary and 2) possible. It's necessary because as we break up with what's broken us, we have to replace those old thoughts, patterns, and perceptions. It's possible because we have both God's grace and allowance for repentance and redemption and His fruits to replace them with. Granted, I understand this soul cleansing seems more difficult than other forms of change, like a juice detox for example. Changing what's in your fridge is less difficult than changing what's in your heart and head. Nonetheless, change is necessary. You know who else heard that line? Andy Sachs.

This relatable character from *The Devil Wears Prada* reminds us of just how awkward a transformation can be at first. Stumbling her way into the fashion industry, she learns through Nigel, her fashion guru of sorts, that her look needs its own alteration. If you've seen the film, you know how magical this scene is.

Can you imagine?! If Stanley Tucci opened those double doors to a closet filled with diamond-laced dresses and Jimmy Choo shoes for me, I would retire my credit card altogether. What need is there to shop when your work closet is better than your personal closet could ever be?

But Andy didn't become a fashionista until she stepped into those Chanel boots. She didn't master a model's walk until she wore more designer brands than most models can afford. By putting on the clothes, she also put on a new air, a new confidence, a new mold. She knew nothing about styling before she took the job and had no qualifications to be at one of the leading fashion magazines, but by being immersed in the atmosphere and putting on the clothes, she came to not only understand fashion but also to be fashionable.

Sometimes we need the outfit change to see our true potential, or in our case, our true identity. We need to be immersed in the *right* atmosphere. We need to put on the accessories and attributes of who we're becoming.

Too often when it comes to our future growth and our relationship with God, we think we must have it all together and fully understand Him before we're allowed to take a step forward. We might say, "Gotta get my life together before God will accept me for the job He has in store." "Have to look the part before I can take the part."

God's storehouse is far larger and grander than that double-door closet. Similarly, though, it's full of divine items that change and elevate us when we put them on. His storehouse is stocked with the fruits of the Spirit: "But the fruit of the Spirit is love, joy, peace, forbearance, kindness, goodness, faithfulness, gentleness and self-control" (Gal. 5:22–23). Just as easy as we can run to the grocery store for real fruit, we can run to God for the fruits of the Spirit. We're able to "put on" these fruits, and as we do, we no longer see our old selves in the mirror. Instead, we see who we're becoming.

What habits do you need to leave at the door?

What atmospheres and communities are fueling these habits?

Ask yourself those questions as you embark on this growth journey. It will help you continue moving forward uninhibited and unstoppable. Change doesn't have to be daunting or compli-cated. The mold we want to make of our future selves is developed through the bending and breaking of certain parts of our lives. We must allow God, the Great Sculptor, to knead and fix as needed to bring about His completed work.

Michelangelo worked on the statue of David for roughly three years, continuously shaping the details. Interestingly, the most significant change was in the beginning. Michelangelo sculpted the masterpiece from a slab of marble that had sat untouched for twenty-five years.[2] Many artists had given up on the material being a beneficial piece of art and deemed it unusable for a sculpture. But Michelangelo carved and changed the once-useless stationary block, transforming it into the famous Italian piece thousands travel from all over the world to see today. In this case, the biggest disservice to the original marble block was not changing it at all. It sat void for a quarter century because no one saw the potential hidden within. Through its evolution, its significance and purpose were unveiled.

And we all, with unveiled face, beholding the glory of the Lord, are being transformed into the same image from one degree of glory to another. For this comes from the Lord who is the Spirit. (2 Cor. 3:18 ESV)

The idea of being unveiled represents an underlying splendor so magnificent, it's unlike anything the world has ever seen. Moses veiled his face after being in the presence of the Lord because it was too radiant for the other Israelites (Exod. 34:29–35). Paul wrote this verse in 2 Corinthians to show that when we look to Christ as our example, we, too, have faces like Moses's—brushed by God's glory and marked by something more. From glory to glory, we shine.

Do not be afraid of change. It may feel awkward or uncomfort-able at first, but there is beauty behind the process of breaking the former mold. With open hands and open minds, let's further journey into the conversation of change and growth.

We cannot accept more until we free ourselves of our less.

Character Development

No matter what movie genre you gravitate to, nearly every film made has a common element: character development—the method used to evolve your favorite silver-screen stars during the course of the story.

This is typically achieved through external or internal conflict. One of the most common types of conflict is man versus man, when two people are at odds, such as in *Macbeth* or the Harry Potter series. Another type is man versus fate, with quest plots like we find in *The Odyssey* or The Lord of the Rings series. Yet, in any of these conflicts, the main character is the driving force of the story. They are the focus throughout.[3] Rarely does a character go through a major event or trial without growing or learning from it.

We are the main character of our own life's story, and it's essential to be aware of our character development.

I'm a recovering passive aggressive-ist. Growing up, if something bothered me or I felt irked, I hid it deep down. My hurt or anger would fester inside until my mind filled with perfect comebacks, motives I imagined the other person held, or a belittling backstory. It was messy and draining handling problems that way.

During my engagement to Arden, our disagreements exposed my passivity in conflict. I'd struggle to express how I felt and shut down. It embarrassed me and frustrated him. But over time, I learned and grew from it. The same processes that once limited me now liberated me. Good conflict in marriage isn't human nature. If we're honest, we enjoy being right and fight to gain the upper hand. It's easier to shut down or blow up than it is to vulnerably express ourselves and patiently listen to our spouse. But what's better? Tallying a win for yourself or creating a win for your marriage?

The truth is, it's always going to be easier to simmer in our thoughts, wallow in our shortcomings, and stay in our comfort zones. But we're much better off letting people into the depths of who we are and giving them permission to journey with us on this path of transformation. We need to open up to someone—our spouse, parent, or best friend. Let's not keep people at arm's length. We don't need to keep score, we need one another.

I've often heard people say, "I want to have strong relationships, but I won't be with anyone who tries to change me." I applaud those who can stand up for being true to themselves. But for those who say they'd rather be alone than deal with change or conflict, I implore you to see what's fueling those reservations you carry. In regard to my own behavior, I was so scared I was unlovable that I kept others away before they had a chance to prove me right, or I'd shut down when things got hard because I thought if I lost control, they'd see the worst parts of who I was. I was lacking intimacy with those most important to me because of internal insecurities I couldn't let go of.

We can't stay friends with the insecurities that keep us from intimacy with those we love.

We can't stay friends with the insecurities that keep us from intimacy with those we love.

I believe we have gotten to this point of being absolutely terrified of someone changing us—our friends, our mentors, our partners—because we struggle with our identity. Once we grasp a part of our self that feels solid and true, the thought of any change related to that part feels like someone pulling the rug out from under our feet. That one piece of identity has become our foundation. Has anyone ever suggested a form of change to you, and you instantly became defensive, offended, or upset? Was that change tied to something you truly believed about yourself?

Sometimes people's advice is helpful, while other times it's not. There are two vastly different versions of relational change: selfish gain and empowerment. Someone who sees who you are and says, "That's not enough, so let me change you into who I want you to be" is after selfish gain and control. Someone who says, "I see you for who you are, and I see even more potential and depth within you that I will commit to bringing out every day" is after your best self.

We must remember that growth is a product of change. We can equally embrace who we are today and still move toward growth, also known as *changing*.

There are two definitions of change I want to highlight. The first is the one I believe we most commonly associate with the word—"to replace one thing, person, service, etc. with something new or different."[4] According to this definition, the need for change can cause us to feel replaceable, defective, or less than. It can make us ask, "What was wrong with me before?" "Why don't you just accept me as I am?" This view is limited and hinders our potential; it focuses on our present self and forgets our future. That's why it hurts so much. We set ourselves up to receive any feedback under this definition as an insult and to view the person bringing the change to attention as being on the offensive. However, when change is approached in a helpful and healthy manner, it takes on the second definition: "to make somebody/something different."[5]

Different isn't always bad. Sometimes different is an elevation, upgrade, or transformation. Take the dynamic of a trainer and trainee, for example. This is a relationship that benefits positively from change. An athlete who has worked hard to get where they are may seek help from a trainer to enhance their skills. If they want to become the best in their field, the trainee may have to make changes based on their trainer's advice regarding their eating habits, techniques, and/or tendencies. But what if the trainee were closed off to change? Would they achieve what they were expecting? Most likely not. They could do drill after drill, but if they ignored their trainer's advice, they wouldn't grow. It would be a waste of the athlete's time, talent, and money.

Change is helpful when those in our corner are looking out for our best interests. Whether it's a coach's critiques, a boss's constructive criticism, or a spouse's caring counsel, heeding advice from those we trust benefits us.

Now, just because someone's advice is beneficial doesn't mean it's always easy. According to an article published by Training ABC, "Using criticism constructively is one of the most difficult emotional intelligence skills to develop. It's easy to react negatively to criticism. However, by carefully examining criticism, you can find ways to improve yourself. . . . Remember you cannot control the negative emotions that criticism brings, but you can control your reaction to them."[6]

I used to be closed off to change, especially professionally. I'd hold my work with clenched fists, feeling if anyone altered the direction or offered suggestions, it threatened my ability or expertise. I even saw this in my marriage. When Arden would offer opposing direction about something personal, I felt I had to defend my ground. I slowly saw the pattern. I was resistant to change because it felt like admitting I was wrong or less than. Ultimately, I believed that if others saw areas for growth in me, that meant they saw me as lacking. But what I felt wasn't what was true.

If we are constantly defensive toward suggestions from others, there could be a reason. Recall the lesson from chapter 5 that shame and pride coexist. Pride (too high an opinion of one's own ability or worth) keeps us closed off to change. Because the more we fixate on how we appear to others or what others think of us, the more shame can twist our peace, leading to insecurity, distrust, and agitation. In this state, others' words have a skewed undertone we create in our heads. But if we remain humble and open, we reap the benefits of their feedback.

People are either catalysts or blockades to our growth process, depending on our response. King Solomon, deemed one of the wisest and richest men in history, had much to say on the matter of counsel:

> The way of a fool is right in his own eyes,
>   but a wise man listens to advice. (Prov. 12:15 ESV)

> Listen to advice and accept instruction,
>   that you may gain wisdom in the future. (Prov. 19:20
>   ESV)

Seeing something, even ourselves, from someone else's point of view can unlock secrets to our potential we may not have discovered otherwise. If we held all the keys to our own growth, there would be no need for relationships. But because iron sharpens iron, another bit of wisdom credited to Solomon, friction is required to grow stronger. We need others to help raise us to higher standards and point out the things we can't see within ourselves. We know who we are and who we want to be, but we are still blind to some things within us. If you don't believe me, just get married. You'll see things within yourself, good and bad, come to light by being in proximity to someone else.

Though it's not always comfortable to uncover untapped potential within ourselves, it's much more painful to wake up one day and realize parts of us have lain dormant for years. I think I can speak for you and me both when I say that we'd hate to be that marble lying dormant for years but would love to be a prized art attraction. Let's get to chiseling away what covers the masterpiece underneath. I invite you to welcome three Cs for change: crew, cravings, and currency. Chip by chip, we'll chisel down to the good stuff—together.

Change Your Crew

I wouldn't consider myself a NASCAR fan. I think I'd get a little dizzy watching hours' worth of left turns. But I do applaud the drivers' focus and the diligence of their teams. I don't know much about the art of racing, but I do know that if you asked Jeff Gordon or Danica Patrick if it matters who's in your crew, they'd say yes. A NASCAR pit crew has seconds to do to a race car what it takes a dealership hours to do to your Toyota. A pit crew's actions can be the determining factor in whether a driver wins the race or finishes second. As three-time NASCAR Cup Series champion Darrell Waltrip says, "The amount of work and coordination that goes into a successful pit stop in NASCAR is astounding. In just a few seconds, the entire course of the race can be changed."[7]

I want to finish well. Not in a car race; I wouldn't bet on myself in that situation. I want to finish well in life. At the end of the last lap, I want to see a smile on God's face as he tells me, "Well done, good and faithful servant" (Matt. 25:21). Good and faithful. How do we know we're on track and continue to run the race ahead of us well? One vital piece of the race is our crew. If a driver needs a pit crew to help keep them on track for a few hours, how much more do you and I need the right crew to help keep us on track for years? Ask yourself these questions:

Who's in your crew?

Who refuels you when you're low?

Who helps you assess what's going well or what's going wrong in your life?

Who do you share the important times and decisions with?

Are any of the members in your crew slowing you down?

Just like in a race, the right crew can make or break how you finish. The people in your inner circle help steer your decisions and actions. They rub off on you in multiple ways. Now, hopefully unlike a pit crew, you're not paying your friends to be on this journey with you but you are choosing them wisely.

> The righteous choose their friends carefully,
>   but the way of the wicked leads them astray. (Prov.
>   12:26)

This is one of those bits of wisdom that can seem harsh or alienating. We don't set out to create our own microbubbles with only people who think or act like us, nor do we toss people to the side if they have any struggles or flaws. However, there is a difference between our peers and acquaintances versus our inner circle and closest friends. Jesus loved everyone—Jew or gentile, educated or uneducated, sinner or religious—but He confided and invested in few.

We need a close-knit group. The people we do life with, our ride-or-dies, our besties for the resties. The people who will call us out when we need it, cry it out when we're hurting, and stick it out to the very end. So I ask again: Who's in your crew?

The people you've chosen are the ones you've allowed to know your personal intricacies. Essentially, you've brought them into the laps of your life, hoping they only take you farther. As you work together as a team, your goals should align, and you should work well together and celebrate and share wins.

As you think of the people who are pouring into you, if they feel more like competing drivers or far-off spectators, it's time to change your crew. If your girlfriends are always on the hunt for the wrong guy and bringing you to prowl with them, they're not setting your tires in the right direction. If your closest gals talk only about themselves and never take time to care for or check on you, they're not refueling you. If your best buds make your goals their competition or are constantly dragging you down, they're creating damage instead of assessing it.

If you want to finish well, you can't afford for your crew to be misaligned. In any relationship—friendly, spousal, or working—you need to be on the same mission. Simon Sinek stresses the importance of aligned goals and thinking even in the business and consumer relationship by stating, "The goal of business should not be to do business with anyone who simply wants what you have. It should be to focus on the people who believe what you believe."[8] The obstacle in misaligning our most important relationships is the chance we'll get slowed down, our travel will run off track, or we'll wear down on the journey.

Remember those moments of brokenness and regret from chapter 2? The times we found ourselves asking, "How did I end up here?" I'll bet at least one of those moments was in some way a result of or somehow correlated with spending time with the wrong friends, boyfriends, or communities. Again, we shouldn't avoid being friends with those who see things differently from us—those friendships can be huge areas for growth or restoration. But when we desire to have a set vision, keep certain morals, or engage specific practices, our choices must reflect said desires—that includes our choice in our crew.

Another activity I don't foresee myself participating in anytime soon is bungee jumping. I simply do not have a desire to be a human yo-yo. If I suddenly had a wild hair to be reckless or I lost some significant bet and the consequence was bungee jumping, I'd choose the best, most secure, tested, and proven bungee cord known to humankind. Because if I ever jumped, I'd want to finish back on top, not splat on the ground. The secure bungee and I would be on the same mission: to not break anything during the jump. But the already fraying bungee and I would not.

We can't trust people on missions different from ours to safeguard that we'll get to where we're going any more than we can trust a fraying bungee cord to get us back up after a jump. It wouldn't be safe for us, and it wouldn't be fair to them. The people you entrust with your well-being and essentially your heart should always have your safety in mind.

You may be thinking, *Christian, it's not that deep.* Isn't it though? The average person spends around 210 hours with friends per year (yes, that average includes us introverts and parents).[9] That's enough time to influence the way we act, think, and speak. Your crew *will* change you. If they're not changing you for the better, it may be time to change your crew. As Paul told the Corinthians, "Do not be misled: 'Bad company corrupts good character'" (1 Cor. 15:33).

A social study out of Michigan State University found that the importance of friendship on health and happiness only continues to grow as we age.[10] If you commit to developing the right crew now, you'll spend a lifetime changing and growing into your best self. What's beautiful is the friends who make up your crew have also chosen you to be on theirs. Jointly, you aid each other as you are all on a mission to run well the race set ahead of you.

The right crew allows the entire team to finish well. It creates a band of intentionality, integrity, and accountability—all of which are needed to finish well.

We can wish to be successful, pure, faithful, motivated, or fit, but none of these are achieved by wishing on a star—they require action. When we invite a special core group of people into our lives, we get support we can rely on. Our crew keeps us accountable. They act as coaches who won't allow us to give anything but our all, a support group when our goals seem too far away, and a guardrail when we're wandering too far. Are your people calling you to a higher standard or just calling you to hang out in places you shouldn't?

Change Your Cravings

My body is worth more than what I crave.

I confided in you about my former delicious but unhealthy habit of diving into an Edwards Chocolate Crème Pie without restraint. If I did that today, my stomach would punish me for a good day or two. My body has become used to a more natural diet and an overload of sugary, artificial food would leave it, and me, wondering why I ate what I did. It's just not worth it, no matter how good it sounds during a craving.

Something that looks appealing to the eyes might hurt the stomach later because our eyes deceive us. When we don't respect the balance our body was designed to handle, we put it at risk. If we consume protein, greens, and fruit throughout the day and then enjoy some unrefined chocolate dessert after dinner, we're enjoying a balanced diet. But if we flip that equation and indulge in sugars and sweets all day, then add half an apple in the afternoon, we create an unbalanced diet and probably wouldn't enjoy our choices that night, if you know what I mean.

We have to be knowledgeable about what we're taking in and what's good for us.

That pie sure looked good enough to eat, and my eyes said, "Sure, you can eat this entire pie," but my stomach knew better, especially after the first time. But my eyes and stomach didn't always communicate clearly. Those days I was doing a tiny bit of modeling, and I tended to eat like a bird on the days I had a shoot, then pig out when I got home.

Why do we crave? Cravings aren't bad. But what we crave gives us indications about our health. In my case, my undereating amplified my body's need for calories, and my stomach screamed CHOCOLATE! I'd tell myself, "I've hardly eaten, I can spare the calories!" But despite what our teen magazines told us in high school, counting calories isn't the way to look or feel our best.

Foods we crave may sound good in the moment but often become decisions we regret later. The same is true for what our flesh craves. Desire can deceive us. That's why we need to understand what's behind our yearnings ahead of time. If we're hungry but on our way to dinner, we'll be less impulsive when we see the Krispy Kreme hot light on. But if we're driving around aimlessly with a hungry appetite, we're more likely to pull over for a fresh glazed doughnut.

We want it, we crave it. It seems good in the moment, but realization seeps in when the act is complete. "Well, that wasn't what I was expecting. Why do I feel unsatisfied, incomplete? Maybe I shouldn't have done that. I don't like this feeling."

I've also noticed that when I eat a nutrient-dense meal, I know when to stop. I eat until I'm full, not until the "I'm going to be sick" point. Truly, how often do you hear someone say, "Man, I ate way too much salad, but I just couldn't stop myself"? On the flip side, it's more common to hear of overindulgence and blurred lines of satiety in correlation with unhealthy food and drink—sugars, alcohol, french fries, etc. When we are satisfied and our bodies have received the nutrients they need, we feel full. Here lies another spiritual correlation. When we are filled with the things of the Spirit, we won't overindulge on the things of the flesh.

He who is satisfied loathes honey,
But to the hungry soul any bitter thing is sweet.
(Prov. 27:7 AMP)

If we're looking for love in the wrong areas, we will not find it. We *will* find, however, its cheap substitutes—the counterfeits that claim to satisfy those cravings. Think of it again like what we eat. Take a stroll through any grocery store, and you'll find hundreds of foods with the labels "no sugars added" or "low fat" and assume they're healthy options. But are they really? The American Heart Association conducted studies and found that some of the products with "reduced sugar" or "lightly sweetened" claims actually had more sugars, carbohydrates, or saturated fats than alternatives with no claims—concluding that it can be misleading to make a decision about a product based on a package claim.[11]

How much simpler and healthier would it be if instead of opting for variations, we sought the real thing? I know I've talked about nutrition extensively, and while I hope you do take care of your heart from a dietary stance, my primary goal with this chapter is to help you take care of it through your spiritual well-being.

We cannot look for variations of love; we must go for the real thing. Variations harm us down the road and do something dangerous in our mind. These substitutes—from romantic flings to insatiable habits—make us believe we are taking in what we need even though we aren't. When it comes to the way we live, we must have a no-substitutes mindset.

We hear people say, "Oh, there's no harm in doing this or watching that," but the danger is hidden within.

Our world has been indulging in lust, porn, and casual sex for so long, I'm afraid many people can no longer identify the pain these things cause. These substitutes for love have skewed our hearts' satiety, and we have forgotten, or never truly learned, what it means to be filled. Like children who ate only chicken nuggets and PB&Js, we've grown up on a cheap spiritual diet and think it's nourishing us, when in truth, it's feeding *off* us.

The more we feast on bad cravings, believing they're "okay," the more our taste will be attached to a longing that is ill-fitted for what we actually need. This is why we must change our desires to see different results.

Sometimes we excuse our diet by saying that eating healthy is just too hard or expensive. Been there, said that. But once I changed my eating, I saw that my excuse wasn't accurate. I'm no organic cooking guru, but as I expanded my palate and knowledge, my taste buds changed. I used to eat only strawberries and preferred them dipped in chocolate. But now I include the rainbow in my diet: pink peaches, orange carrots, yellow squash, and green spinach. Once I ditched the excuses, I found I wasn't as picky as I'd thought and eating healthy was not as hard as I'd imagined. It was a beneficial switch that started with a simple commitment to change.

Eating healthy doesn't help you only look better; it makes you feel better. How is this so? Because your stomach is your defense. Your gut houses somewhere between 70 and 80 percent of the cells that make up your immune system.[12] When your stomach is out of whack, your health is too. Could it be that obvious with our fleshly cravings too? Are we as motivated to get the good stuff and lay off the bad? They say a good way to break up with your bad cravings is to detox. I bet if we detoxed from our unhealthy cravings of the heart, we'd also find a stronger defense within our spirit.

Change Your Currency

There are 180 currencies around the world. If you visited a foreign country, be it Italy, Brazil, or Turkey, your US dollar wouldn't get you far. One of the first things you'd see in the airport, after you made it through the long customs line, is a currency exchange center. That's because you can't get very far with a wallet full of another country's currency. It would be like going to your favorite coffee shop, ordering a delicious latte, then trying to pay with Monopoly money. Unless a sympathetic barista pitied your confusion and said, "Bless your heart, honey. It's on the house," chances are you probably wouldn't walk out caffeinated. Monopoly money doesn't work in the real world.

What currency are you using? Not in your purse, but in your mind. Thoughts are like money—they're worth a little or a lot, depending on the system you use. Our systems of logic and reasoning can be worthwhile or worthless. Positive thoughts are profitable while negative thoughts are not. Which currency do you tend to use?

Currency 1: negativity, pessimism, overthinking, stress

Currency 2: positivity, optimism, rational thinking, peace

Each currency is prone to a different return. What we spend our thoughts on often yields what we deposit. Cash a negative thought and gain a negative outlook. When our world itself is broken, it's common to respond with broken thinking. But if we want to have a positive, profitable life, we can't let our surroundings determine our currency. When we feel burned out, bummed out, or like we want to break out in tears, it could be due to negative thinking. If we want to see change in our lives, we must change the way we think.

As I write this, for the first time in twenty years, the euro is worth less than the US dollar.[13] So if you fancied a trip across the pond, your dollar would be worth a little bit more. But there's an even better exchange rate benefit in changing our negative thinking to positive thinking.

When we exchange our negative thinking for positive, Scripture-based thinking, we receive a far better return. We gain an increase in our outlook, joy, and overall well-being. As we eliminate damaging practices like negative self-talk and entertaining what-ifs, we find a brighter horizon in our minds. Positive thinking not only helps our mind feel less clouded, but it also opens us to even more profitable ways of living. Research has shown positive thinking may have the following benefits:

- Increased life span
- Lower rates of depression

- Lower levels of distress and pain
- Greater resistance to illnesses
- Better psychological and physical well-being
- Reduced risk of death from cancer, infections, and respiratory conditions
- Better coping skills during hardships and times of stress[14]

I want the above attributes in your life. Your thoughts have value, and if you allow yourself to toss out the negative in exchange for the positive, you'll see a beneficial impact.

Burn, Baby, Burn

In early 2019, Arden and I went on our first ministry trip together. Our friend Mattie Montgomery invited us out to Fresno, California, to be a part of the Altar Conference. From the moment we landed, we saw lush palm trees and witnessed incredible miracles. When we learned we had a free day, we thought, *Why not add to the adventure?* We looked for something neither of us had ever done. We couldn't find anything at first, until we scanned farther outside of Fresno. Then, there it was. The thing that was just simple and crazy enough to do with the few hours we had. We threw on the Cali-weather appropriate clothes we had packed, shorts and tank tops, and headed to Yosemite National Park.

It was just over an hour's drive away. After some time passed, the palm trees faded into pines, and our excitement level rose. Neither of us had been there before, but we had both seen pictures of the lush, giant sequoias.

When we reached the forest entrance, I was stunned by what I saw, or didn't see. There were no green leaves swaying in the wind, only black bark staring blankly back at me. "Forest fires must have swept through here not too long ago," Arden said at my visible disappointment.

He told me a story he remembered about the California redwood trees. After nearly 10,000 wildfires one season, a group of scientists researched the impact of this surplus of fires and found a particular generation of redwoods that had been growing poorly prior to the fires but were now thriving. Up until that point, the wildfire team's technology had become so advanced at catching fires that many redwoods weren't exposed to fire at all. This was a huge advancement for wildlife and nature. But much like human beings, trees can be surprising.[15]

The scientists discovered that the more this generation of redwoods was guarded from fire, the less the trees reproduced. A layer of natural debris and plants covers the forest floor, preventing the trees' seeds from reaching the soil and taking root. But when the forest is exposed to fire, that layer burns, revealing the seeds and allowing the trees to reproduce. These trees are quite literally creating beauty from ashes. We've marveled at their beauty for ages, but perhaps we can also learn from their story.

It must be a common theme for the men in my life to inspire me through fire and trees, because I once heard a similar thing from my father. Dad owns a few acres of property down in our sweet home Alabama, and once on a visit he asked me if I wanted to accompany him and burn the land. Half concerned my father had become a pyro and half disturbed he thought me mischievous enough to join him in the lunacy, I asked why on earth he'd do such a thing. He assured me that this was not an act of arson but of renewal. A controlled burn on a wooded area removes dead leaves and tree limbs and reduces insect populations. The right kind of fire can be rejuvenating.

Just as the redwood scientists had gotten so good at evading fires, we also have become good at avoiding the fires in our lives. When we come up against a situation or person that could hurt us or a tension that seems too invasive, it's easier to steer clear of the flames. But in doing so we limit our development. I see our own personal growth so much like the seeds of those redwoods. For protection, we shelter ourselves with our own type of covering layer. If you have any area or behavior in your life that makes you want to run away, isolate, or rant on your social media—that's your covering layer.

These are not the same as boundaries. Boundaries are developed as safety rails for the benefit of maintaining relationships. Covering layers are put up as protection to keep others at bay. You can liken it to a gate versus a wall. Gates protect while still allowing openness and visibility. Walls, however, conceal and communicate to others to stay out.

A covering layer could manifest as your being guarded, passive-aggressive, or offended. Our desire to control our environment and circumstances may keep us from pain or discomfort, but it will also hinder us from growth. However, if you are brave enough to endure the friction of change, you will grow.

I'm not saying we should text everyone in our contact list and ask what's wrong with us. I'm suggesting we be open to helpful conflict and healthy change.

If you are brave enough to endure the friction of change, you will grow.

The first few months after our wedding, Arden and I had our own fires we had to brave in order to grow our marriage into the kind we both envisioned. We were two people coming together to be one, and that meant sorting through anything that got in between our bonding. That kind of growth required us both to be honest with ourselves and each other. Was my selfishness keeping us from creating the gracious partnership I sought? Was his stubbornness keeping us from connecting well emotionally? These were questions we had to ask.

I've often heard the expression "If you're not growing, you're dying." I think this is just scary enough to make us want to lean into the tension of growth instead of staying still. In our relationships, our hobbies, and our self-journey, the idea is that we must keep going. There is nothing wrong with where we are, but if we become complacent, we forget there's more ahead. Our purpose is a path of discovery. We can grow without being afraid of who we've been. We can look forward to change without denying who we are. Growth is simply taking a step in the right direction and continuing to keep going, one foot in front of the other. Second Timothy notes that when we ask God to cleanse us, He enables us to shine for Him. Like a diamond forged through the flames, the refining fire He leads us through does not destroy or burn, but it does reveal our purest and loveliest inner workings.

> Those who cleanse themselves from the latter will be instruments for special purposes, made holy, useful to the Master and prepared to do any good work. Flee the evil desires of youth and pursue righteousness, faith, love and peace, along with those who call on the Lord out of a pure heart. (2:21–22)

Only God could take our impurities and make them flawless. It's an equation that will never make sense—our worst for His best. Yet Christ ratified the exchange. He looks at you as the most precious prize ever created and out of adoration asks, "Will you allow me to remove that hard layer that's limiting you from growing to your full potential?"

THE
BREAK
THROUGH

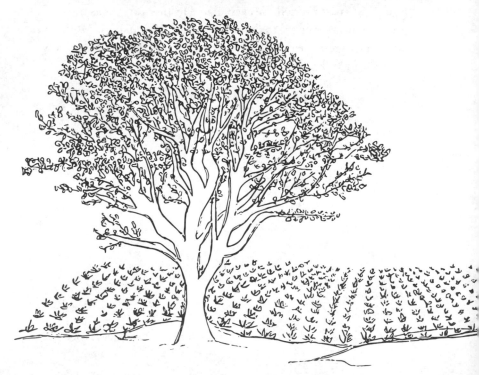

Part 3

Gather the garden.

Tend to the harvest of your heart—autumn abounds.
Make way for what is emerging, rising from the grounds.

Years of darkness rectified in a moment;
The enemy never stood a chance against such a worthy opponent.

Trading our less for what He deems best,
wisdom leads the righteous; those immersed in new wine.
Shame's chains unfastened; our identity repossessed.
I am my beloved's and He is mine.

People shall say, "Hasten your stride; you'll want to see,
the glory that shines from the face of the redeemed!"

The land that laid waste has become like Eden,
bursting through the floors and rising to the ceiling.

You are fashioning.
You are blooming.
You are declaring.
You are flourishing.

Allow His Word to drip from your head to your heart.
Let the light break through—all along you were set apart.

10. Your Prince Charming Is Waiting

The shape of true love isn't a diamond. It's a cross.

—Alicia Bruxvoort

Much of my adolescence was spent on the water. When I tell people I was raised in Alabama, they picture a little girl on farmlands in her cowgirl boots riding horseback. And while that was part of my childhood, more often we spent the weekends enjoying the island of Gulf Shores, cruising the waves and watching dolphins' silhouettes in the sunsets. The ocean is a mystical treasure, and I cherish the time I spent growing up around it—especially during those hot Alabama summers when the heat index broke one hundred degrees and it was revitalizing to jump right into the water.

But have you ever been swimming when the water was chillier than you'd expected? Then you take a different approach. You dip your toes in first, trying to inch your way into submersion, but the frigid shivers rush through your body before you can convince yourself to go a step deeper. If your circulation is on the slower end like mine, you may decide in that moment you're okay with letting the water win this round and yell to your friends, "It's too cold. I can't do it! Just go on without me." Then one replies, "You have to go all in, head under—just jump!"

As bone-chilling as the idea is, you know they're right.

Continuing at our toe-dipping rate, it'll be an hour before we get all the way in—if we do at all! When we feel timid or weary, we tiptoe in. But when we go all in, in that head-under position, we override second-guessing and dive straight into the experience.

In fall 2021, Arden and I celebrated our third anniversary by traveling to Italy. Our first stop on the itinerary was the magical Amalfi Coast. If you've ever been to or seen pictures of the area, you know about the turquoise waters that crash along the coastline of colorful buildings, the natural winding hills and pristine beaches, and the crafted cuisine of pleasant pastas and lush lemons.

On our first day, we took a boat tour around the island of Capri, famous for its dancing waters, notable blue grottos, and coveted panoramas. Coasting over the waves was breathtaking, but it was also a rather brisk October day. The skipper showed us some of Capri's beautiful shores and gave us up-close looks at the grottos. He dropped the anchor and offered the chance for us to swim.

As you might imagine, not everyone jumped off the boat at once. Many of us had sweatshirts and blankets wrapped closely around us to block the chilly wind while cruising. Knowing my husband's adventurous nature and desire to enjoy experiences to the fullest, I leaned over and asked, "You want to jump in, don't you?" He simply smiled. I knew, even if no one else did, that my scared-of-nothing husband was going to dive in. Capri is a once-in-a-lifetime experience, so my cold-averse self needed to weigh which was more important: my current comfort or the regret I'd have at not being able to tell our future children how Mom and Dad swam in Capri's blue grottos. So, with trepidation, I shed my comfortable layers and mustered up enough courage to walk to the edge of the boat and begin the count: 3 . . . 2 . . . 1 . . . JUMP.

As soon as I hit the water, I looked at Arden frantically and said, "I have to go back!" I had never jumped in water so bone-shakingly cold! But that Colorado native I married, having a better understanding of cold shock than I did, grabbed my hand and said, "Go head under and all in." In my frigid, frantic state, the last thing I wanted to do was get more of my body wet. My head was the last thing holding any ounce of warmth left in my body! But part of this whole married thing is trusting each other, they say, so I forced my teeth-chattering mouth to pause and held my breath. Then I dipped my head, which was full of ways Arden was going to make this up to me, under the water. To my surprise, I felt warmer.

In tandem, we swam to the grotto and saw the vibrant colors dancing from the ocean floor and reflecting on the caverns' ceilings. We were the only ones who jumped in. But you know what? We got to experience something sensational up close that the others could only see from a distance. Not everyone decides to go all in. As I look back, I know it was worth shedding the comfortable to experience the wonderful.

Your relationship with Christ is much the same—an invitation for something meaningful, *if* you're willing to shed the layers of comfort and forsake the status quo. Don't let cold feet keep you from meaningful moments. Maybe you've never fully said yes to God, or you've been a Christian for a long time but realize you haven't gone ALL in. When we tiptoe into the waters, dillydallying in the shallow end, we don't feel the full effect. Jumping in may seem to isolate you—making you the only one jumping off the boat, if you will. You may have your own cold shock, thinking, *What am I losing by going all in and what are others going to think?*

I'm thankful Arden was my advocate for going all in, calling me to go deeper than I was comfortable with or thought I was capable of. I'd like to be yours now as you go all in with Christ. Even more than a trip to Capri, your relationship with Him is a true once-in-a-lifetime experience.

Going all in is the first step in declaring our life has changed from brokenness to wholeness. He's the One who touches our broken pieces and, with His master hand, constructs them to be fully operable and divinely beautiful. We cannot declare what we don't have, and until we go all in, head completely under, we're still tiptoeing the waters of our faith. But once we take a big breath, let go, and fully immerse ourselves in Him, He rushes over us like a wave, refreshing us with a heavenly fullness.

True Freedom

Some people refuse to go all in because they think they'll have to trade their freedom for a religious set of rules. Could that be your hesitation too?

It's a situation I like to call "Faith FOMO." That's when you love Jesus and can't wait to spend eternity with Him but don't want to miss out on life before then. Social media hasn't made this condition any less prominent. With so many filtered selfies and lavish escapades, there's frequently the idea that the Christian lifestyle is void of the ability to enjoy life.

That's because we equate freedom with free choice. As teenagers, we believe we'll be free when we are out from under our parents' roof. As women, we think we'll be free when we have the right to govern our bodies without input or opposition.

People who live free from rules feel they can do as they please without a second thought. They have the freedom to do it all because the rules don't apply to them. But what's hidden in the fine print of this life is that everything, even if done "freely," comes at a price. Every action we take follows the universal law of cause and effect. We may have the freedom to do what we wish, but we don't do it without consequences. And sadly, the things that cost us the most considerable consequences tend to offer the least sufficient warnings.

This "YOLO" lifestyle offers zero restraint up front, but its choices catch up to us. On the contrary, abiding under a system of rules, say the law or the Word, creates more barriers up front but grants more gratification. I'd argue we are not forsaking freedom of choice but using our freedom to choose wisely. So, you tell me: Which way is truly the most freeing?

Adopting the Word as a way of life is relying on wisdom higher than our own. I've lived doing whatever I wanted and I've lived according to God's instruction, and let me tell you, the latter offers more freedom than the former ever could. Because Christ went ahead and paid the consequence on our behalf, if we repent and follow His example, we find the way to true life, and in like manner, to true freedom. Today I am free from shame, free from sin, and free to live a life I am proud of. The same can be true for you.

> How much more, then, will the blood of Christ, who through the eternal Spirit offered himself unblemished to God, cleanse our consciences from acts that lead to death, so that we may serve the living God! (Heb. 9:14)

Why Jesus?

There are many methods that promote the soul healing we desire. Therapy, manifesting, horoscopes, meditation, and yoga are just a few. We are hungrier for something bigger than ourselves and more willing to believe in something we can't see than we'd readily admit. It stems from the deep desire within to know and be known by our Creator. To this end, dubious searches for meaning resemble those bad ex-boyfriends we mentioned before—lost causes. If we attach our soulful longings to something powerless or adverse, we'll be left still wanting.

But how do we separate what's real from what's relative? There are over four thousand religions worldwide. It's not just hipster, new age Gen Zers who wonder, *Who am I and what do I believe?* People in America and Saudi Arabia alike desire to find their purpose. All the aforementioned methods lack a vital component for transformation—Jesus Christ. So the question present is this: Why Jesus?

I was asked this question point-blank.

Back in college, I was waiting tables near closing time at a restaurant one night and began what would become a theological conversation with a professed unbeliever. I was exhausted from my shift, but I'll never forget the words we exchanged.

The man said that although he didn't believe in Jesus, he was a good person, and after studying many of the people he knew who attended church, he saw more kindness and generosity in himself as an unbeliever than in those who professed to believe. What was the point of going to church if doing so resulted in no noticeable difference? My heart broke a little at his words, and in that moment I felt a little sheepish. It's true—people can be kind and do good on their own. Going to church doesn't always make someone a saint. With these thoughts circling my mind, I asked myself the same question he asked himself: "Why would anyone be prompted to believe in Jesus?"

All I could muster in response was what I knew to be true despite those unsettling thoughts. "I believe you're a good person, and there's truth in your examination. But I also know that no matter how 'good' your life is externally, if you don't have a real relationship with Jesus on the inside, then you're missing out on the best part." Half expecting a condescending chuckle or retaliatory answer, I was surprised as he responded with, "Oh . . . I've never heard it that way before."

If church is just a building, then we will just be attendees.

If charity is just a donation, then we are just do-gooders.

If Christ is just a role model, then we are just fans.

But we are not justified by our "justs." If we want to feel more, be more, and live more, the ways we perceive and interact in this relationship must change. It is the most important one we will ever have.

The personhood of and dependence on Christ is what separates Christianity from every other doctrine or ideology. To stand out in this world, we must share that dependence. Let's refute the unspoken perception that going to church and reading the Word every so often is substantial—that's how we become a "good Christian," right? To illustrate, I can post a photo of my family on Instagram every day saying I'm #blessed yet only spend mere minutes with them in real time. I love sharing photos of moments with my loved ones because those moments are fueled by relationship. I post because I love them, not as a way to prove I love them.

My early years of faith had a lot of those superficial hashtag moments. I went to church wearing my Sunday best but often still felt my worst. I was near the building but far from God. In the Bible but out of touch. Though I outwardly acted like a devoted follower, I was lacking a genuine love for God. This was because I didn't yet understand His love isn't something I earn or put on; it's a gift. His sacrifice wasn't to hold something over our heads while fixating on our flaws, but rather, it was for relationship. Our outward expression is only the surface level of our relationship with Christ. Genuine connection happens deeply.

We can go through life on our own and get through seemingly okay, maybe even better than average, and we can say we believe all we want, but the power, love, and freedom of faith come in having a relationship with Jesus. The revelation that Christianity was less about religious rules and more about relationships changed everything for me. Jesus went from a man in a robe I'd heard about in Sunday school who I had to please to the Son of the God who was pleased with me. Everything changes when we see that Christ isn't just *the* answer but *our* answer. He's our

Jesus went from a man in a robe I'd heard about in Sunday school who I had to please to the Son of the God who was pleased with me.

answer to our purpose, our identity, our transformation, and our salvation. Why follow Jesus? The answer, *our* answer, is within the question.

Loved You at Your Darkest (Circles)

My husband loves my punching bags. Maybe I should call them what they really are—my dark under-eye circles. I love that my genetics gave me high cheekbones and olive skin, but I was never a fan of the dark circles I inherited. I remember bringing my mom the proofs from my first-grade picture. She had curled my hair, put me in a spring floral dress, and was thrilled with how cute her little girl looked. I frowned and pointed to the picture. "But it looks like I got punched in both eyes!" From that day forward, I referred to them as my punching bags.

I hoped one day I'd grow out of them or tan enough that they'd better blend in. When those methods proved unsuccessful, I moved on to creams—drugstore brands at first, then the expensive items. Nothing worked. I'd have these things forever. Come on, how can some girls get away with no makeup? They don't know how good they have it! I, however, didn't leave the house without concealer for years. No way was I risking getting the distressing "Aw, you look tired!" comment.

There's the joke that we girls never let a guy we're interested in see us without makeup. Then he'd know we're not the flawless, airbrushed lady we catfished him into believing we were. Let's give men more credit than that, ladies. When I started going fresh-faced around Arden, I thought he'd be kind and tell me I was pretty or I didn't "need" makeup, as men are obligated to when they say "I do," but I never dreamed he'd say more than that. One day when I was makeup free, he doted on my cuteness and I unbelievingly pointed under my eyes and said, "Yeah, except for these punching bags!" He stopped, looked me dead in the eyes, and said, "I love your under eyes. They're part of what makes you, you!"

That isn't the only time he's said something of the sort either. He always flirts when I feel I look my worst and makes adoring comments about the parts of me that I wrote off as undesirable long ago. It's shocking when someone loves the pieces of us that we thought were design flaws. And if we're honest, it's scary to first step out to see if we will be received. If they'll catch our heart or stomp on it. But what does that say about the love we accept and the designer Himself?

It's almost baffling that someone would love our dark circles and beauty flaws, but more so that a perfect God could love us despite our darkest inner flaws. Still, Romans 5 makes that un-thinkable idea an unbelievably healing reality.

But God shows his love for us in that while we were still sinners, Christ died for us. (v. 8 ESV)

His love is not away from us. He doesn't hide us. He doesn't love us only when we're picture-perfect. Like my husband's true love for me covered the dark areas I'd been covering with concealer, God's love for us covers what we've been concealing in our lives. If we try to hide parts of ourselves or pretend we're someone we're not, we keep a piece of ourselves from God—one He's already covered with His love.

The Bible tells us how God designed us intentionally. If God Himself is love (steadfast and unconditional), and we were made in His image (pristine and without mistake), then His love covers every inch, every wrinkle, and every shortcoming. He is in and over all His creation, covering every square inch of you and me alike—internally and externally. His method of love extends to every area of His creation, whether seemingly beautiful or flawed. The Master Designer does not make design flaws, and His store-house has no shortage of material for His design.

Activating the gift of grace requires us to first admit we need it. What is the purpose of paying a high price for a tool you have no use for? How much power does that same tool have if it sits on a shelf? There is power in looking shame in the face and saying, "You no longer have power over me because the power of the cross reigns supreme."

Repentance is not an admission of guilt tied to capital punishment; Jesus already took care of the latter. It's a confession that frees us from the shame and subjection that sin brings. That tight balloon that's been in your chest for far too long, that pains you with the inability to breathe freely, can be released. You don't have to live that way a second longer. Because Jesus's sacrifice on the cross eradicated shame for all.

Pinpoint everything you've carried, then pause and imagine this: God pulling that heap of shame, anxiety, and regret from your bones and handing it to His Son on the cross. Christ looks at you, then to His Father, and says, "If this cup cannot pass by, but I must drink it, your will be done!" He takes it willingly, but not without pain. At that moment, you give away all of what destroyed you to create room for all He gives to free you. His sacrificial death is also the death of your shame. You watch as He bears the pain that was yours. And as He breathes His last breath on that cross, you take your first without pain. God turns back to you and says, "Daughter, you are now free."

> *At that moment, you give away all of what destroyed you to create room for all He gives to free you.*

Jesus did more than save us from hell; He released us to freedom—true emancipation from the shackles of our past that kept us tied to who we once were. This is the demonstration of 1 Peter 5:7, "Cast all your anxiety on him because he cares for you." He invites you to silence shame and cast it all to the cross because He so deeply loves you. He has a better life, a higher way, and a new identity awaiting you.

Will you trust Him and His process?

Think back on the best teacher you had in school. Recall what was exemplary about them and how their teaching impacted you. One of the best teachers I had was Mrs. Ramirez. She was patient, offered support, and truly believed in her students. She transformed the classroom from a lecture hall to a place for open thinking that allowed us to take ownership of our growth. When we struggled to grasp a concept, she probed us to see where our thinking was misaligned. And when we asked for help, she worked with us to get to the right answer.

Now imagine God as your teacher. This life is our classroom, and He invites us into the growth process. Our small view of God assumes He's a teacher who only wants to tell us what to do and critique us when we're wrong. But He's not. He helps us grow constantly, and when we begin down the wrong path, we have the availability to repent and call out to Him, "God, I did this wrong; I need your help."

When we repent, we are frankly saying, "Lord, I need You." He doesn't want to punish us for messing up. He wants to lend His power and strength to help us climb higher. I think back to the concepts I learned and that confidence I gained under Mrs. Ramirez as I went on to college to receive my bachelor's degree. In the same way, I think back to all the milestones I conquered when I repented. Repentance is simply turning from the dead end we started in and getting back on track with God's plan.

I've learned a little something about getting back on track. My original due date for this manuscript was days after my son's due date. I'm not sure why I agreed to birth two major valuables in the same period. It was probably because I underestimated how much both would require in the last few months while my body was requiring more rest. But while Azariah arrived a little early, my manuscript was now late. My wonderful editor encouraged me that to stay on track, she should start reviewing the beginning chapters as I completed the rest. "NO!" the perfectionist in me wanted to scream. It wasn't complete yet; there were still so many rough areas. I was worried she'd crumble the mess up and toss it out completely, just as my college professor did in front of our entire class years before. I had to present perfect or nothing.

But my editor wasn't my professor. She worked with me through the realities this new season had brought and encouraged me to keep writing. She didn't toss my story in the trash; she reviewed it and advised me so I could finish it successfully. If I had held on to this book until it was free from error, it wouldn't be in your hands today. I had to let go of that past pain that made me believe perfecting by myself was the only option.

God also isn't a lecture hall professor. He doesn't expect you to have it all figured out, with every *i* dotted and *t* crossed. He doesn't give you an ultimatum: be perfect or don't bother. Like my editor, God wants to help make your story the best it can be. He wants to cut out the dead works and dead ends to get you on track with the beautiful ending He has for you. Turning in my chapters let my editor help me improve this story; turning to repentance let God improve my personal story.

Repentance allows God to redeem and rewrite your story.

Admit you need His guidance. Don't hold back because there are spots you want to scribble over or white out. Instead, hand them over to Him so He can work His magic. As He redeems and rewrites your story, you may discover how much good was buried beneath the excess that needed to be removed.

Digging with New Tools

What type of vacationer are you? Are you the mom of the group who is the go-to for everything? Or the spontaneous one who books a flight the week of? Or maybe the overthinking fashionista who needs three suitcases "just in case"? I'm the planner, through and through. Because I'm a control freak? Hmm, maybe slightly . . . but I plan mostly because I want to be fully immersed in the places I visit. How do I know the best restaurants to dine at without a little Yelp research prior? How do I find the best exhibits a city has to offer unless I scout them before the trip? There's some method to my madness, as planning allows me to get the most out of a trip—whether we're going to Six Flags or the Sistine Chapel. I feel what we learn in advance advances the experience. So before we visited Pompeii, I did a little reading on the preserved city's history. I was shocked by many aspects: the surprisingly vast size of the ruins, how obviously the people's sexualization had influenced their architecture (look that one up on your own time), and how much we're still learning today about the town that was destroyed nearly two thousand years ago.

Amedeo Maiuri was a lead archeologist who uncovered many remnants of the city in the 1960s, including one of the most sobering exhibits on display today—the Garden of the Fugitives. You hear the word *garden* and imagine green grass and budding flowers, but remember that this land was destroyed by Mount Vesuvius. Maiuri and his team found partial skeletons of thirteen people who had tried to evacuate the city, so they created plaster casts to depict how they may have looked before they were asphyxiated by the volcano's ash.

After making the thirteen molds, Maiuri created a backstory for the group members based on what archaeologists had discovered and could gather. He decided this group contained three families: two of farmers and one of merchants. Within the families he noted that the children had all been fairly young, some accompanied by slaves, and the group themselves had been lower-class citizens. How fascinating to not only uncover but also have some insight into the humanity behind these remains. Well, the problem was that due to the limited archaeology technology sixty years ago, Maiuri and his team could only base so much of this story on evidence and left much to speculation.

In 2020, archaeologist Estelle Lazer and her team took on the task of continuing Maiuri's work of uncovering the real lives behind these preserved Pompeii plasters. Lazer, with her upgraded medical imaging technology and methods, was able to push past the limitations Maiuri faced sixty years prior and base her synopsis on more fact than theory. What Lazer and her team discovered would disrupt the narrative formerly held.

The backstories Maiuri had created for the Pompeii natives did not align with the modern bone scans and linked artifacts Lazer found. The team concluded that these individuals who got left behind were not fugitives, slaves, and paupers but were in fact families, artisans, and people of middle-class prominence.[1]

It's amazing what taking the time to rediscover can do to the entire narrative. Through the process of uncovering, the stories of these thirteen residents of Pompeii were redeemed. Have you labeled yourself a mess up or ruined because of your past? Keep digging deeper. You are not a mess up; you are made new. You are not ruined; you are restored. The previous narrative you believed about yourself is no longer accurate. Like with the backstory of the Garden of the Fugitives, new advances (Christ's intervention) have redeemed your story.

> More than that, we also rejoice in God through our Lord Jesus Christ, through whom we have now received reconciliation. (Rom. 5:11 ESV)

What's amazing to me about the story of the fugitives is that Lazer's developments didn't change what happened before. These people had still been declared "less than" for years, until Estelle's discovery rendered such past statements void. In the same way, our journeys of betterment don't change what we did or experienced in the past, but Christ's intervention renders them void.

He sees our true worth and invites us to live from that place.

Cinderella was invited to a better place . . . literally. The beloved storybook character, whose true name is Ella in some adaptations, was by law included in Prince Charming's formal guest list because it extended to every eligible maiden in the land. But because Ella's stepmother deemed her "less than," she treated the girl like a servant and kept her busy with duties considered shameful so she wouldn't believe she was worthy of a prince. It took her fairy godmother intervening to open her eyes to the truth that she was welcome and wanted. But even then, she couldn't go in her ragged state. The kingdom was a place of splendor and majesty; it was inappropriate for her to arrive in her tattered garments. No, she needed to leave her soot-stained attire behind. As the story goes, her fairy godmother removed her rags and replaced them with exquisite fabrics and adornments fit for a royal ball. The godmother's makeover was no doubt magical, but what else did this encounter change for Ella besides her wardrobe?

Perhaps Ella's internal transformation was even more marvelous than her external one. Think about how she grew up hearing that she was inferior to her siblings, answering to the demeaning nickname "Cinderella," which translates to "little ashes." While her sisters were prized, she was put to work. That type of family trauma would typically require more than a pretty dress to resolve. If I were in her shoes, those beautiful glass slippers, I'd be more taken aback by the fairy godmother's remarkable kindness than her magic. Imagine believing for so long that you were less than and suddenly someone comes into your life and shows you in a lavish way that you are seen, special, and sought after. Well, take away the wand, and you have a wondrous example of Christ's outlandish love.

I believe that when we give our lives, our hearts, our past, our *all* to Jesus, He removes our rags and redeems our true identity. In an instant, we are transformed. The old is gone and the new has come. Now, through His great love, we enter His royal kingdom as His children, His heirs!

> You will be a crown of splendor in the LORD's hand,
> a royal diadem in the hand of your God. (Isa. 62:3)

After the ball, Ella didn't return home the same. She was marked by this encounter. When Ella's stepmother tried to hold her back and hide her away once again, her new, awakened authority arose within her, and she finally broke free. When her future came knocking on their door via the king's messenger, she stepped forward to claim the destiny awaiting her with a tailor-made glass slipper in hand.

Once you've released your past and shame to Him, you must break open the doors that held you back in the first place. You, too, are awaiting a future of splendor through Christ. He sees you as a royal diadem, a prized possession polished and purposed for His glory. This is not a fluffy, feel-good statement—this is your destiny. You are a chosen instrument and part of a royal priesthood (1 Pet. 2:9).

The diadems we're familiar with are crowns and tiaras. They mark power, nobility, and status. I believe this destiny will be a banner over your life. As you break up with what broke you, sweeping the limitations and skeletons of the past behind you once and for all, you can look forward to the future and find the splendor of being a daughter of the one true King.

God is guiding you; stay the course. The permanent way to live in the peace Christ has given us is to get out of the old habits that led us down a path of brokenness. And that's exactly what we're going to do in the next chapter.

He gives us a new name and a new identity. We are no longer broken, or susceptible to breaking, but in Christ we are whole. He has rewritten our stories and removed all the broken editions that do not belong. Spoiler alert: He has written redemption into *every* chapter, weaving it all together for a better ending. The question I ask you now is, Are you willing to uncover your testimony to fight for your breakthrough?

11. You Have a Testimony

If you give it to God, He transforms your test into a testimony, your mess into a message, and your misery into a ministry.

—Rick Warren

A bullet, a bus, and a breakthrough.

When Malala Yousafzai began fighting for girls' education in Pakistan, she was just a girl herself. Around that time, over 7 million Pakistani children were out of school and 58 percent of those were female.[1] In her region of the Swat Valley, Pakistan, the Taliban was the biggest obstacle to girls getting an education. The radical group banned young girls from attending school because they believed their place was at home and out of sight.[2]

Malala's campaign for equal education didn't sit well in a nation shadowed by extremist thinking. One day, at the age of fifteen, she boarded a school bus, only to wake up nearly four thousand miles away at the Queen Elizabeth Hospital in Birmingham, England.[3] After she boarded the bus, a member of the Taliban boarded too. Calling the young girl by name, he opened fire, sending a bullet into Malala's left temple. The bullet grazed her left eye, skull, and brain, damaging her facial nerves, eardrum, and jaw joints.

Facing literal brokenness in her body and a broken spirit, what was the young activist to do? What would her story be after this brokenness entered the narrative?

Malala didn't begin activism on a whim. Her father, Ziauddin Yousafzai, led the very school she attended, Khushal Girls High School and College in the city of Mingora. It was a center committed to educating and equipping young women. Her father saw women as cherished, capable people worth fighting for. His influence led Malala to stand up for girls' education, and I believe it also helped her stand back up after she'd been knocked down.

She endured and overcame.

After numerous surgeries, Malala took up her cause again, this time with the support of leaders and organizations around the world. Her bravery did not go unnoticed. She was named one of *Time* magazine's most influential people in 2013 and became the youngest recipient of the Nobel Peace Prize in 2014. Malala said, "We realize the importance of our voices only when we are silenced."[4]

Today, her testimony has inspired millions. Her father continues to stand by her side and fight the cause. The father-daughter duo created an organization, the Malala Fund, to continue the work of furthering girls' education not only in Pakistan but around the world. The Malala Fund works for a world where every girl can learn and lead. At the time of this publication, the fund had raised over 22 million dollars to further female education.[5]

You, too, have a testimony—one that needs to be shared. Your heavenly Father is right by your side, equipping you to share it. Let us learn from Malala's words. If our testimony is a vehicle for breakthrough in our lives and others', then we cannot afford to remain silent.

Not Only for You

Finding and sharing our testimony is important because it's not only for us.

The enemy didn't sneak into the garden simply to fill Eve's mind with destructive thoughts, and he didn't riddle us with shame just to mess with our mind. Those shameful scenarios replaying so faintly that only we can hear them make it seem like we are the sole target of the enemy's torment. But he knows that if shame can drive us into an isolated battle, our defenses are weakened. Believing we are backed into a corner fighting by ourselves, we fail to see the arena surrounding the ring. It's filled with both those cheering us on and those who are watching to learn how they can fight their own battles—those who can testify that we are more than conquerors and those who will look to our testimony for how to conquer.

Your breakthrough will change your life *and* the lives of those around you. Whether you're a verified Instagram influencer with a little blue check by your name or you barely check your phone because you have little ones constantly calling your name, your testimony is impactful.

Surrounded

I was lucky enough to receive an athletic scholarship to college and continue playing the sport I loved. Tennis was my outlet for mental and physical strengthening my first two years of school. But when I transferred to Auburn University to complete my bachelor's degree and had to start a new fitness regime, I quickly realized how much more I enjoyed sprinting in a tennis game than I did running merely for my health.

I was not a long-distance runner. The monotony of the treadmill paled in comparison to the drive I felt competing on the court. When my stamina began dropping, I needed a new way to push myself. So I did what any former athlete would do for some ambition: I got an audience and adopted a motivational motto. I began running around campus because I knew if I was tempted to give up midstride, I'd push myself harder in front of onlookers. When I felt all eyes were on me, I remembered Hebrews 12:1–2:

Therefore, since we are surrounded by so great a cloud of witnesses, let us also lay aside every weight, and sin which clings so closely, and let us run with endurance the race that is set before us, looking to Jesus, the founder and perfecter of our faith, who for the joy that was set before him endured the cross, despising the shame, and is seated at the right hand of the throne of God. (ESV)

This became a life verse for me over the next few years. So much so that I printed it on the back of my running shoes as a reminder that even when I didn't feel like continuing, I was running for a reason. Now, I know Paul wasn't writing to encourage college girls to run with endurance to avoid the sneaky freshman fifteen, and physical fitness wasn't the only reason this verse stuck with me. These were formative years when I started to understand the significant burden I'd allowed shame to build in my life. It was a weight I couldn't shake off no matter how many miles I ran around Auburn. This required a different endurance.

Individual breakthrough allows for collective benefit.

Recounting that first line, "Therefore, since we are surrounded by so great a cloud of witnesses," I awakened almost from a slumber to the reality that my path didn't only affect me. I wasn't on this journey alone. In the same manner that seeing others along my running path encouraged me to go farther, realizing that how we run our race influences others' paths gives us endurance to keep running on the path of our purpose.

Breaking up with what broke you will undoubtedly add a pep to your step as you leave the nagging voice in the dust, but I believe in the motto that you can only run *from* something for so long; for longevity, you need to run *to* something. Running just to run ends when you begin to tire. But by running with a destination or a divine destiny as your focus, you can push through the shin splints and remember you're on a path. Persistence and pain both need purpose.

You and I are in that same arena—surrounded by a great crowd of witnesses, including those who have gone before us to pave the way and those who will follow. The Bible ties believers together—both young and old, neighboring and foreign, new in faith and faithful for years—as one body. Our God-given purposes align to function together like conjoining bones and ligaments. Though important on their own, together they generate movement and power.

Individual breakthrough allows for collective benefit.

What are you running to and who is watching? You're on a path, whether it's overcoming addiction, raising children as a single parent, or leaving a toxic pattern or relationship, you have an end goal in sight. You're also influencing an audience, whether it's your siblings, your roommates, or your coworkers, people are watching how you run the race. Many sports teams spend time watching footage of their past games and meets to make sure they're performing well. Take a second now to note how you're running the race ahead of you. If you feel like you're losing momentum or languishing, reset your gaze on Jesus.

Influence Others

> And they overcame him by the blood of the Lamb, and by the word of their testimony. (Rev. 12:11 KJV)

Notice the subject in this verse: they. *They* overcame through testimony. Without a second thought, we share our favorite TV show to binge-watch or that killer sale at our favorite store. We're not shy to share what we enjoy or the benefits we've received from an object or experience. So let me place this thought out there: What if *our* testimonies aren't really *ours*?

Perhaps your testimony can affect and transform all those around you. God's wondrous power on display is a sight to marvel at. Your life redeemed and reworked is His masterpiece, a more beautiful display than prized art in a gallery. Don't keep such majesty tucked away—showcase the delight that has the power to transform!

A favorite pastime of mine is surveying art museums. To me, they're a marvelous journey through history. Some exhibition pieces cost well more than you or I will ever make in our lifetime. For example, the current highest-selling painting is the *Salvator Mundi* (Savior of the World) by Leonardo da Vinci. But, surprisingly, this piece has an outlandish variation in its last two sale prices.

Now, I'm not talking 2022's shocking housing market price jumps. I'm talking more! According to an article published by *Vanity Fair*, the piece sold in 1958 for $60.[6] No, you're not reading too fast. I'm still talking about the same prized painting! That's because at the time, it was thought to be only a copy of the lost da Vinci original painted by Bernardino Luini, a follower of the famed artist. The painting was rediscovered and restored in 2007 and relocated to the Metropolitan Museum of Art, where critics and scholars studied the piece and noticed that the master craftsmanship of the strokes belonged to none other than the brilliant da Vinci.

Can you fathom the increase in value our testimonies hold when we share them?

When its authenticity was revealed, its value rose astronomically. At a 2017 auction, a company of interested buyers went back and forth for nineteen minutes raising their paddles in competition to own the piece. The winning party was an Arabian prince who cashed out at $450 million for the piece.[7] I told you—more than we will likely make in our lifetime!

What can we determine about the correlation of shared experience and value? If the *Salvator Mundi* had been kept tucked away for private viewership, its legacy would still equate to a mere $60. But after more people saw and experienced this piece, its value rose by a whopping 750,000,000 percent. Can you fathom the increase in value our testimonies hold when we share them?

We hinder the value of our stories when we keep them to ourselves. Over time, they'll collect dust, lose significance in our minds, or become forgotten altogether. We can even begin to forget the original Artist of the masterpiece, buying into the deceptive thought that perhaps it was all our own doing or our own exaggerated imagination. *Am I really a new person, or has adequate time simply passed since my last mistake?* I need you to take the wonder off the shelf, remove the canopy. Remember, the *Salvator Mundi* was painted not by da Vinci's follower but by da Vinci himself! Your story is not your own inconsequential design from a lowly follower of Christ; rather, your story is the masterful working of the Master Creator!

> Salvation is not a reward for the good things we have done, so none of us can boast about it. For we are God's masterpiece. He has created us anew in Christ Jesus, so we can do the good things he planned for us long ago. (Eph. 2:9–11 NLT)

Recognize the significance in what God's done through you, not solely for your benefit but for the benefit of all! The Bible is laced with testimony after testimony showcasing God's redemptive power. Each account paints a different display of how our God can take the seemingly mundane, the sometimes easily discarded, or the visibly flawed and, through His reconciling grace, make a remnant more radiant than a Rembrandt.

> It has seemed good to me to show the signs and wonders that the Most High God has done for me.
>> How great are his signs,
>>> how mighty his wonders!
>> His kingdom is an everlasting kingdom,
>>> and his dominion endures from generation to
>>> generation. (Dan. 4:2–3 ESV)

Let the redeemed of the LORD say so,
whom he has redeemed from trouble. (Ps. 107:2 ESV)

There have been countless moments when I was fighting fear but hearing another's testimony fueled the fire of my faith. When we reveal our testimony, we share the mystery of the gospel and the transformation of grace. Our testimony gives legs to the faith others are contending for, allowing them to walk in belief. Share what God has brought you through. Because your testimony is not only what you've experienced but also *how* you live.

Live In Such a Way

Paul writes,

> Meanwhile, live in such a way that you are a credit to the Message of Christ. Let nothing in your conduct hang on whether I come or not. Your conduct must be the same whether I show up to see things for myself or hear of it from a distance. Stand united, singular in vision, contending for people's trust in the Message, the good news, not flinching or dodging in the slightest before the opposition. (Phil. 1:27–29 MSG)

I love that Paul uses the verb *contend* here. It's a declaration that requires effort and assertion. We contend for people's trust in God's message with our character and conduct. Our lives are on display as we are His hands and feet. It's our joy and responsibility to showcase His goodness and care for His people. Through our actions, character, and speech, we reflect our hearts and the One who lives inside them.

It's been said that hurt people hurt people. Then what if redeemed people lead people to redemption? The Bible says, "I planted the seed, Apollos watered it, but God has been making it grow" (1 Cor. 3:6). I believe that once we've seen a miraculous transformation in ourselves, God invites us to be a part of someone else's experience.

Plant and water seeds.

Live in such a way that showcases that growth is possible. Live in such a way that invites people into the mystery of grace. Live in such a way that authenticity and honesty remove shame's foothold. Because how you live matters.

Do not for a second think your testimony doesn't carry weight.

I want to denounce the idea that your life has to mirror someone else's to be significant. We grow from others' testimonies, but don't get stuck trying to fit your story into their book. Our role models help mold us, not make us fit in their mold. Remove the saying "I'll never be as impactful as ____" from your vocabulary. If you focus on being the next "big name," you're going to chase someone else's legacy instead of finding your own. God doesn't make clones or carbon copies. His purposes for us, His children, are as unique and specialized as His love for us.

If Christ leaves the ninety-nine to find the one, then even if your testimony impacts only one person, it is worth living. I don't know who led Christine Caine to the Lord or who testified to Priscilla Shirer that women can preach, but would we know the impact of these women's purpose if the ones who went before them had abandoned their calls and instead copied someone else's? Our breakthrough and decisions have a similar grandiose domino effect. We must live our testimony so that we may become all we were created to be and walk in the purpose and authority Christ bestows on us. I want to see you set free *and* carrying the invitations to others' freedom.

Second Corinthians 5:20 says, "We are ambassadors for Christ, God making His appeal through us" (ESV). This excerpt declares that you and I have been reconciled with God for the purpose of being His and bringing His beloved to know Him. We have been graced with the gift of shame eradication from the perfecter

Do not for a second think your testimony doesn't carry weight.

of faith. But the narrative doesn't stop there. With this gift, we are entrusted to a ministry of reconciliation. Now, ministry in this sense doesn't mean what you might think. Ministry is not only a vocational career but also a way of living and relating. God's not asking you to quit your day job and start a church tomorrow—or maybe He is, and if so, that's a wondrous purpose! But what *ministry* means is spreading the good news that Christ made a way where there was no way for all who call on Him in faith.

As daughters of Christ, we experience the greatest rags-to-riches story ever told, and we must not keep silent. We are partakers in the miraculous and ambassadors for its expansion. We must never let our minds dwindle into the realm of small thinking or casually regarding what He's done and what it means.

Romans 10:17 notes, "So faith comes from hearing, and hearing through the word of Christ" (ESV). I'm eternally grateful that Jesus's sacrificial love wiped the dust from my brow and made my life beautiful, and I'm grateful to be able to testify of His redemption so that other women may be awakened to the restorative love of God.

We must speak so others can hear.

Our generation has become loud in sharing "our truth" or "our story" but quiet in sharing the truth in our testimony. But your story is not what's happened to you; it's what God has done for you. My story is not that I was a lost, lovesick, anxious person, but that God redeemed me from longing through His unconditional love.

I Like Big *Buts* and I Cannot Lie

But is the most exciting word in the Bible, and not because it reminds us of Sir Mix-a-Lot. Anytime you see the word *but*, you know God is rolling up His sleeves and getting ready to interrupt the former narrative to do something big. Just look at these *buts* (emphasis added):

- "*BUT* in your great mercy you did not put an end to them or abandon them, for you are a gracious and merciful God" (Neh. 9:31).

- "With man this is impossible, *BUT* with God all things are possible" (Matt. 19:26 ESV).

- "You were dead in your transgressions and sins. . . . *BUT* because of his great love for us, God, who is rich in mercy, made us alive with Christ" (Eph. 2:1, 4–5).

- "Once you were not a people, *BUT* now you are God's people; once you had not received mercy, *BUT* now you have received mercy" (1 Pet. 2:10 ESV).

With His *but*, God saves the lost, finds a way where there was no way, revives His people through grace, and brings the lost and lonely into a family of believers. These testimonies of the Israelites, the Ephesians, and the Asian province are all wrapped in the truth that God redeems His people. God, being the Word and the Truth, flips the narrative on the brokenness in our lives and in the world to rescue His people for His glory. When your testimony is tied to the Truth, it will have a big "but."

I was lost, BUT now I am found.

I was weak, BUT now I am strong.

I was hurt, BUT now I am healing.

I was broken, BUT now I am breaking through.

Don't be afraid to show people your but. (This is *not* an endorsement for streaking! Please don't quote me if you're arrested for indecent exposure.) This *is*, however, a plea to share the miraculous work God has done in your life! The enemy would love to silence the truth in your story. And with a little cunning ability, he attempts to sow a seed of timidity to bury the seeds you're called to plant in the lives of others.

Remember, the enemy is an accuser. His bag of tricks is lined with deceit. He'll likely tell you that your story doesn't matter to anyone else or that it's trivial. If you've attempted to share your testimony in the past, you may have felt a relapse of shame, fear of postponed penalty, or an undeniable lack of confidence that stole the strength from your words. If that's happened before, it's okay. Your testimony might be the key to someone else's breakthrough. Don't listen to the accuser or the butterflies—keep sharing! Remember what our key verse says? "They *overcame* . . . by the *word* of their testimony" (Rev. 12:11 KJV, emphasis added).

We overcome by speaking. Don't let the accuser steal the seed you're called to plant. My hope is that as you experience breakthrough and wholeness in Christ, you'll be an advocate of hope through the message of your testimony, helping other women break up with what broke them and avoid settling for halfway healing.

> We will not hide them from their children,
>   but tell to the coming generation
> the glorious deeds of the LORD, and his might,
>   and the wonders that he has done. (Ps. 78:4 ESV)

As ambassadors of reconciliation, we have the privilege and duty to model how to walk in the fullness of Christ. Remember the woman at the well from chapter 5? Your testimony is a gift—one you'll want to share with others. After all, they say sharing is caring, right? Let the accuser's lies fall void here. As your friend, let me tell you this: you have come so far. The things that attempted to break you did not leave you powerless; ultimately, they made your story powerful. There is someone who needs to know that God is good and they are not without hope. The truth from *your* testimony, the words from *your* lips have the power to harvest God's miracles in another's garden.

Malala's story didn't end at brokenness but, rather, led to fighting for her breakthrough. I'm thankful for your journey and your strength. Use your voice. Trust what's within. This is just the beginning!

12. Nobody's Damsel in Distress

A powerful woman is a heat-resistant and storm-bracing cali-
bre. There is nothing she cannot handle.

—Gift Gugu Mona

One of the most popular tropes for novels for centuries has been
the damsel in distress. Medieval stories centered around noble
feats and heroic protagonists typically painted female characters
as damsels in distress. According to the Oxford Dictionary, a damsel in distress is a young woman in trouble, with the implication
that the woman needs to be rescued, as by a prince in a fairy tale.
According to the Cambridge Dictionary, a damsel in distress is
"a young woman who is in trouble and needs a man's help."[1]
Historically, women in this trope were sexy but senseless, sweet
but silent. They were doomed to live a life of misery or pettiness
until some robust man in plated armor could finally find his way
to her in the third act of the story. Even when they were the main
characters of their stories, damsels in distress lacked the qualities
needed to overcome what they faced and seal victory—identity,
intelligence, and independence.

You're not a damsel in distress—you're a heroine in the making. You're the woman who slays her own dragons, outwits the enemy, and braves the unknown. Now, that doesn't mean you can never accept help or you're against female empowerment if you get married. It means you're more than a prize at the end of someone else's path. Marrying my husband was one of the best days of my life, but he isn't the source of my identity—that role is solely reserved for my Creator.

God doesn't rewrite our story to work us into the background. He restores us to our initial glory.

> Before I formed you in the womb I knew you,
>   before you were born I set you apart. (Jer. 1:5)

The only Savior we need is Christ, and He never makes us wait on Him to fight some monster before He saves us—He's already won that fight. God gives us every asset we need to be victorious. Instead of leaving us stuck in some far-off tower, He hands us the keys to freedom. Instead of letting us spend our lives in distress, He gives us a spirit of power, love, and self-control.

God empowers us to be females of faith who stand strong in our internal strength, character, and ability. God's girls got grit, y'all! Tell me, who and what more could we truly need outside of Him?

> My flesh and my heart may fail,
>   but God is the strength of my heart and my portion
>   forever. (Ps. 73:26)

Anytime I've faced an overwhelming challenge, I've had to reassure myself with the truth that with God, all things are possible! By His leading and gifting, we can change the narrative and learn how to fight for our breakthrough.

After all, what's a heroine without a battle to conquer? The victories you're fighting for will sometimes require you to roll up your sleeves and get your hands dirty, but the reward for bravery is always beautiful.

Damsels in distress are women in jeopardy with the inability to muster the courage to fight for what they want and need, while heroines use their bravery to overcome the challenges standing between them and their future. They don't wait, they wage war!

Many times, we have an event in front of us that has the power to change our life and the lives of those around us for better or worse, depending on how we respond to it. Will we wait around for someone to come save us or will we lead the charge to enact change?

Often the damsel trope sets the lady in a distressing situation by some form of manipulation. For example, Snow White is fooled with a poison apple, while Sleeping Beauty is tricked into pricking her finger. Ladies, we are not damsels in distress, because we refuse to be deceived! We're no longer fooled by the enemy's tricks or operating with broken thinking. We are fueled by faith! We have everything we need to fight for our breakthrough.

A woman in distress worries and waits in fear. A woman of faith steps forward in confidence because she has hope in the One who has shown her the way of life. We will face lies about our identity, our worth, and our existence, but if we are steadfast in our beliefs, we can identify and dismiss them without hesitation. The sooner we realize the lies, the sooner healing begins.

Ladies, we are not damsels in distress, because we refuse to be deceived!

Remember some of the false narratives I've shared that I had to overcome? That I wasn't strong enough to carry my children or I was too far gone for God to redeem? Each required me to fight to move past them. What narratives do you need to break? In what areas of your life have you felt more like a damsel in distress when you were created to be a heroine?

I want you to be equipped and ready to receive what God has waiting for you, so give one more push. Break up with the false narratives around your life and fight for your breakthrough!

Girl, Get Your Fighting Gloves On

Some people work odd jobs before they begin their lifelong careers. Rachel McAdams was mclovin' it while working at McDonald's for three years. Maybe it was the free Oreo McFlurries that kept the now-famous actress there for so long? Sean Connery's iconic character, James Bond, may have been a hit man who cleaned up after bad guys, but Connery himself got his start as a *milk*man and literal *coffin* cleaner . . . spooky, right? Pope Francis was even a club bouncer before he joined the Society of Jesus.[2] Can you imagine the bishop dressed in white, turning people away with parting verses like, "It is easier for a camel to go through the eye of a needle than for you to get into this club. Bye-bye!"

Odd jobs can bring unexpected destinations. My mom made sure to teach me to work hard and earn my own money for the things I wanted. I began working at fifteen, before I could even drive. I was a hostess at a Mexican restaurant, a children's tennis instructor, and an extra on films. Each of these jobs, as quirky as they were, had their perks—besides the paycheck. The restaurant improved my Spanish, coaching kept me consistent, and films gave me rewarding interactions. I got to be a part of movies like *Guardians of the Galaxy Vol. 2* and the *Divergent* sequel, *Insurgent*.

I can assure you that being part of a movie production is both everything and nothing like you'd imagine it would be. I'll brag on Marvel for being the best company I shot with, both for the great cast and the amazing food they offered us extras.

If you watched The Hunger Games series, you'll recall that Katniss Everdeen's entire journey begins when she volunteers with great vigor to take her sister's place as her district's female representative in the brutal Hunger Games competition. Even though her story is fictional, this character's act takes a great deal of courage. But Katniss doesn't immediately enter the battlefield and claim her victory. After her decision, she is taken to a training facility that requires her to build the strength and learn the skills she needs to compete. We see her advance in her abilities and her tenacity to overcome the obstacles in the competition.

Many of us think there's something wrong with us or that we're weak if we're not naturally #winning at life or if we struggle in some areas. But we must not become discouraged, because it takes time and commitment to gain the spiritual and psychological muscles we need to battle well. If you're working to find your footing or feel you're cornered on every side—congratulations! This means you're right where you need to be to become a holy, war-waging Katniss Everdeen. You've made the decision to fight for more than a mundane life, and now's the time to sharpen your skills.

I have a dear friend I've been able to walk with in her breakthrough journey. It hasn't always been easy. There have been many highs, and right now, more lows. One day she said to me, "I feel like I'm close to falling back into what I walked away from and feel utterly hopeless." She most likely thought I was either crazy or rude as I chuckled in response.

I laughed because I remembered feeling that way—alone in my struggles, under a cloud of doubt and fighting the weight of the world. I told her, "There's a reason you feel that way, and it's because you're taking ownership of your future and developing your faith muscles."

Our old sins don't want to be cast off, and old temptations make a last desperate plea to keep control. Thankfully, we have a God who's right there with us, lending His own strength as we develop ours.

Paul puts it this way as he addresses the church in Corinth:

Everyone who competes in the games goes into strict training. They do it to get a crown that will not last, but we do it to get a crown that will last forever. Therefore I do not run like someone running aimlessly; I do not fight like a boxer beating the air. No, I strike a blow to my body and make it my slave so that after I have preached to others, I myself will not be disqualified for the prize. (1 Cor. 9:25–27)

We are fighting not only for today but also for eternity. Let's stop discrediting ourselves from entering the fighting ring because our feelings tell us we are not worth it. The decision is worth it. The training is worth it. The fight is worth it. Your future is worth it.

Fight through Pain

I have a strange admiration for bees. They're oddly cute to me. Perhaps it's significant to the commotion of this season, as I've felt like a worker bee myself lately, buzzing from one project to the next. But even though I think they're cute, I always admire them from a far, far distance because I know they're venomous. When one stings you, it releases venom through a barbed stinger that pierces and remains in your skin. I always thought that if stung, you should remove the stinger the same way you do a splinter— with your fingertips or tweezers. But if you use that method, you can actually cause further damage.

Apparently, the bee's initial injection releases a surge of toxins that don't fully empty from the barb. Specialists suggest you should scrape the back of a straight-edged object across the stinger to gently slide it out and avoid breaking the stinger and releasing the remaining toxins.[3] Using something like tweezers adds pressure to the stinger and can cause it to break. As if the bee sting wasn't bad enough on its own, right?

Hopefully you're not stung anytime soon, but if you are, now you have this handy life hack. Knowing how to avoid extra pain from a beesting can help us also avoid added pain from the sting of our past. In the last few chapters, I've noted pain points you may have initially been unaware of, but now the wounds are open and throbbing. Your heart may hurt or your pride may be shot. Well, I want to be your "specialist" and help you get rid of the thing causing you pain without further damaging the wound. I haven't experienced a beesting myself (and pray I won't), but I have been stung in life and know healing is possible without having to hurt worse.

When you remove something painful from your skin, you might express relief by saying, "Whew, thank goodness that's gone." *The removal causes us to rejoice.* You may not even know fully how or when the harm happened, but you realized it had to be removed quickly and acted on it. This should be our approach to sin in our lives.

Wounds are painful. We've journeyed through tough terrain emotionally. But it's important that we know how to journey on in strength. That's what I hope the uncovering was to you—a chance to evaluate the damage, clean out the harmful object, and discover how to heal. Eventually, though, the bandage must be removed. When the skin begins to grow back, many health advisors suggest removing all bandaging to air out the area.

Being an overcomer means you may not be at fault or to blame for what's happened to you, but you take ownership of your healing. You release pain and offer forgiveness, many times even when you haven't received an apology. You take control of life instead of letting life control you.

For those of you who have endured abuse, mistreatment, abandonment, or any pain outside your control, I wish I could offer you the apology you deserve. In my limited power, I cannot. But I can stand in the gap and say that you didn't deserve what happened to you and you are worthy of a beautiful future.

God is a good and gracious Father who wants to protect and bless His children. That same alpha and omega Creator knows that pain can strengthen and sharpen us. He lends us His strength, comforts our broken heart, and fights on our behalf. As He undergirds His people in every challenge and hardship, He brings about new strength and new outcomes.

Sometimes miracles are born through trials. The one born in blindness experiences sight at the hands of Jesus. The barren one's womb is opened through the healing of Christ. The one in chains is promoted under the crown. Though we do not look forward to hardship, in the midst of it we can long for the miracle on the other side.

Pain makes us emotional, vulnerable, and human—it urges a homogeneity between us that shows even the strongest have moments. We're all susceptible to heartache or misfortune, and we're all thrust through the door pain opens. As C. S. Lewis writes, "God whispers to us in our pleasures, speaks in our conscience, but shouts in our pain: it is His megaphone to rouse a deaf world."[4]

Fight for Others

Through the biblical book Esther, we see how God places women in positions of potential greatness and how the possibility of achieving greatness lies in our willingness to trust His plan. The woman in this story, Esther, was born an orphaned Jew but later became queen of Persia. She married the king and lived in the royal palace for the rest of her life! Ta-da! The end! That's typically the premise of a fairy tale, right? But it's hardly a worthy representation of the significance in this story.

I don't know about you, but I've grown discontent with the happily-ever-after narrative. Much like the damsel trope, it's superficially short and closes the curtain while there's still more to the story. You're telling me that when a female character rises to power or meets her partner, that's when the story's done? I disagree. That's the start to another chapter, not the end.

See, Esther wasn't born to be a queen; she was born to be a warrior.

Let's unpack some of the important details the above SparkNotes version left out. The Persian King Xerxes handpicked Esther over all the other beautiful maidens in the kingdom to be his queen. She was marked a child of misfortune but crowned a woman of influence.

In the king's twelfth year, he promoted one of his noblemen, Haman, to be his highest official. Esther's older cousin and guardian, Mordecai, was another man in the king's court, and because of this attended Haman's celebratory ceremony. But unlike the other participants, Mordecai, a devout Jew, did not bow down to Haman. (PS: You know God's about to do something in the Bible when a person refuses to bow to another man before God.) This infuriated Haman, who sought an inconspicuous way to punish Mordecai and his people.

> Haman then spoke with King Xerxes: "There is an odd set of people scattered through the provinces of your kingdom who don't fit in. Their customs and ways are different from those of everybody else. Worse, they disregard the king's laws. They're an affront; the king shouldn't put up with them. If it please the king, let orders be given that they be destroyed. I'll pay for it myself. I'll deposit 375 tons of silver in the royal bank to finance the operation."
> The king slipped his signet ring from his hand and gave it to Haman son of Hammedatha the Agagite, archenemy of the Jews.
> "Go ahead," the king said to Haman. "It's your money—do whatever you want with those people." (Esther 3:8–11 MSG)

After reading that passage, it's no surprise that some translations address Haman as "the enemy of the Jews." At the time, Xerxes did not know that his wife was a Jew, and he'd just authorized the mass execution of her family. When Mordecai heard word of this plot, he lamented and urged Esther to plead with the king to retract the command. The only problem was, anyone who approached the king's court without first being called on committed a crime punishable by death, unless the king spared their life by extending his golden scepter. Esther's concerns about approaching the king were valid, especially considering the king's first wife was replaced for an act of disrespect and disregard for the law. Yet Mordecai challenged Esther to awaken to the position of potential greatness she held:

> Do not think to yourself that in the king's palace you will escape any more than all the other Jews. For if you keep silent at this time,

relief and deliverance will rise for the Jews from another place, but you and your father's house will perish. And who knows whether you have not come to the kingdom for such a time as this? (Esther 4:13–14 ESV)

Esther spent the next three days fasting, withholding all food and drink from her lips. On the third day, she entered the king's court unsure what the outcome would be but full of power. As she entered, the king looked on her with favor and extended his golden scepter, saving her life instantly and in effect saving the lives of her fellow Jews in the nation. Hearing his wife's story, the king canceled the decree and turned his attention to the noble who sought to harm his wife's people.

If we break down her name, Esther means "star." She was a beacon of light for a nation, someone on display for her people to shine light in the darkness. However, this was the Persian name given to her in exile. Her true Hebrew name, Hadassah, means "myrtle tree." While studying myrtles and their significance, I found that they were the only representative of their plant family in all of Israel.[5] Similarly, she was the only representative of the Jews in a position to save God's chosen people. For such a time as this, a woman who delighted in and feared the Lord realized her purpose and changed countless lives. She was handpicked by the king to be his wife but chosen by God to be His warrior.

You were also chosen. There is destiny woven into your path and purpose in where you are. God is saying to you now, "Woman, daughter, warrior—it is time to tap into the power I have placed inside you."

Damsels in Distress to Daughters of Destiny

Many know the valiant King David who defeated giants. Some know of his older brothers, the mighty sons Jesse presented to the prophet Samuel. But not many know of his sister, Zeruiah. Like Esther, her name carried meaning too: "pain or tribulation of the Lord." It's not exactly one you're rushing to save for your future baby girl.

But despite the brokenness associated with her name, Zeruiah saw breakthrough larger than herself. She created purpose in places where there had only been pain, using brokenness to birth beauty.

Enduring the pain of childbirth, she delivered three sons: Abishai, Joab, and Asahel, men who became significant warriors for King David. When Goliath's son sought vengeance for his father and nearly killed David, Abishai swiftly saved him. Next, Joab was commander in chief of David's army and often his right-hand man. Finally, Asahel was a military leader under David and noted as the fastest man in the Bible. They were marked by strength, skill, and significance.

While many notable men were known by the region they were from or their father's name, these men were identified through maternal recognition. They were known as the sons of Zeruiah. She didn't allow tribulation to be her end.

Her story shows that struggles cannot steal our strength and pain cannot rob our purpose, but our fight can fuel a legacy. As women, we are called by name to be legend holders. It's often misinterpreted that the Bible portrays women as weak or insignificant, but think about the women we've discussed. From Abigail to Esther, Rahab to Zeruiah, we can see that God intricately destines certain callings for His daughters. We don't need to compare ourselves with men or each other. We share giftings and talents of unique design but use them in different ways.

Her story shows that struggles cannot steal our strength and pain cannot rob our purpose, but our fight can fuel a legacy.

Do not omit the power in your purpose or forget what God has done and is still doing in your life. What battles are you called to conquer? What legacy are you destined to birth? I believe there are battles coming that only we, as daughters of God, can fight. With the weapons God has given us, we will demolish strongholds. Remember you're here for such a time as this moment. I urge you to arise to your true name so that you can become the kingdom warrior you are destined to become.

> "In the last days," God says,
>   "I will pour out my Spirit upon all people.
> Your sons and daughters will prophesy." (Acts 2:17 NLT)

> She is clothed with strength and dignity,
>   and she laughs without fear of the future.
> When she speaks, her words are wise,
>   and she gives instructions with kindness. (Prov. 31:25–
>   26 NLT)

> Charm is deceitful, and beauty is vain,
>   but a woman who fears the LORD is to be praised. (Prov.
>   31:30 ESV)

Daughter is a name of blessing. It's meant not for distress or inferiority but for destiny and importance. God has positioned women as prophesiers, instructors, and faith leaders. We fight for others. We birth beauty and legacy. We are powerful and purposeful.

Broken to Breakthrough

I get girl world. I am the eldest of four girls and eldest cousin of eleven granddaughters and great-granddaughters. But after marrying a man with three brothers and having a son myself, I've quickly become immersed in boy world. Guys say exactly what comes to mind, take less time to get ready, and spend longer than normal in the bathroom. Let the record show that in the average time it takes my husband to "visit the loo," I transitioned to the pushing stage and delivered our son—maybe because I wasn't distracted by football.

Arden is already suggesting we get our son, who is only five months old, LEGOs for Christmas. Apparently you have to start building your collection early. You'd think those little building blocks were of monetary value with the seriousness the male species awards them. I couldn't have guessed how important LEGOs would become in my life, and I know the company's founder, Ole Kirk Kristiansen, never could have guessed how widely successful the company would be when he first began tinkering with these toys.

The Danish businessman wasn't an overnight success. The first few decades of his work were marked by burial. Fire buried his furniture storefront in ash, the 1929 stock market crash buried his plans for expansion, and he had to bury his loving wife long before her time. Sliding into bankruptcy, Kristiansen had to change much in his life, including his business model. He stopped building home goods and turned to a passion for which he was willing to fight despite his lack of funds or the surety it'd work in his favor. He let his background as a builder inspire his creativity. He changed his business model and began making toy building blocks. He reentered the marketplace under the company name LEGO, from the Danish phrase *leg godt*, meaning "play well."

After a few years of persevering through hardships and bankruptcy, Kristiansen's craftmanship of wooden toys began to generate success. But just a few years after he got back on his feet and was finding success with his creations, more burials plagued his efforts. Another fire buried his new workshop, and the strains of WWII buried wood manufacturers' supplies. It was another round of massive blows to his life and work. What was he to do? Keep fighting for his vision or fold under the fires?

Luckily for generations of boys and girls who have enjoyed this man's legacy, Kristiansen decided to keep going. He saw this as an opportunity to adapt and build a bigger and better workshop. He also sought new materials for his toys. He bought Denmark's first plastic-injection molding and began to experiment with creating the first model of LEGO called the Automatic Binding Brick. Like Kristiansen's success, this model took a few years to take off with consumers, but as it did, the toy's popularity multiplied exponentially.[6]

Maybe brokenness was meant to birth your breakthrough.

Today, LEGO has been named the world's most powerful company, ahead of Disney, Nike, and Apple.[7] It's also ranked as the world's most popular kids' entertainment brand, higher than Marvel, Barbie, and Fisher Price.[8] LEGO has held both titles for multiple years in a row. It's safe to say that Kristiansen's fight against the fires he faced proved more than successful. Sometimes the heaviness in our lives that feels like it'll bury us under its pain, weight, or intimidation can actually birth a fighter within us.

Maybe brokenness was meant to birth your breakthrough.

Perhaps you started this book broken—feeling lost or without hope, aspiring to obtain a new strength to heal and carry you through. But little did you know that all along there was a breakthrough within you, just waiting to be unleashed.

For the brave, beautiful women who have gone before us and the ones who will come after, we must commit to walk in the fullness of who we are—breaking the former molds and setting a new example. Walking in fullness is an everyday commitment to see, create, and fight for the breakthrough in and around us. By reflecting on where we started and offering our brokenness to God, we can see His delight made full.

He's been building you up. Like LEGO's legacy was built on what could have broken it, God has built you on what could have broken you. He rewrites your story. He didn't have to wad up and throw away the former pages of your story, and He chose to do something even more purposeful in rewriting them for good. In our transparent state, we offer Him all we have, and He transforms it all into good. He makes the faulty flawless, the painful purposeful, and the broken beautiful. As Charles Dickens writes, "I have been bent and broken, but—I hope—into a better shape."[9]

As you close out this story, I implore you to reread yours with a new lens. Sit with God and process what He's been redeeming and rewriting specifically in your life. What chapters are you reading with a new tone? What subjects are you looking toward with fresh hope? What audiences are you now called to testify to and fight for? As you close this book, I pray you've found closure with the past, you've broken up with what's broken you, and you're ready to leave the less for more.

Acknowledgments

The lessons shared and gift of wholeness itself is fully accredited to God. Thank you to the Creator, who has never forsaken me and has loved me through my own brokenness and led me to breakthrough. What a miracle and privilege it is to be Your hands and feet stewarding Your words and promises through these pages.

I'd like to thank those who made this book possible through their support and/or partnership:

First, my husband, you are a constant stream of joy in my life. You believe in me and inspire me to be the best I am. Your championing, sacrifices, and support have carried this message when I was under stress or unsure. Thank you for being my partner through and through.

To my son, thank you for inspiring me as I wrote this book with you in my womb and for allowing me to share my time with the literary world as I edited the pages with you in my arms.

To my family, thank you for believing in me and this message. My little sister, Brietyn, for being my constant cheerleader; my parents, Marcus and Sonya, for continually reminding me I could accomplish the task; and my mother-in-law, Lisa, for nurturing my creativity and lending your wisdom.

To the wonderful people at Revell and the Fedd Agency, your partnership transformed these words into print. Thank you for furthering this message.

Notes

Chapter 1 What Broke You?

1. Sophie Bethune, "Gen Z More Likely to Report Mental Health Concerns," *Monitor on Psychology* 50, no. 1 (January 2019): 20, https://www.apa.org/monitor/2019/01/gen-z.

2. Kelsey Johnson and Nicole Dienst, "Young People Are Stressed Out All over the World, but Don't Blame the Pandemic," CNBC, June 25, 2020, https://www.cnbc.com/2020/06/25/young-people-stressed-all-over-world-but-dont-blame-coronavirus.html.

3. Brittney J. Miller, "Is the Leaning Tower of Pisa Really Falling Over?," Live Science, July 5, 2011, https://www.livescience.com/33379-leaning-tower-pisa-fall-over.html.

Chapter 2 Broken Moments We Can't Forget

1. J. Kim Penberthy, "Regret Can Be All-Consuming—A Neurobehavioral Scientist Explains How People Can Overcome It," The Conversation, January 7, 2022, https://theconversation.com/regret-can-be-all-consuming-a-neurobehavioral-scientist-explains-how-people-can-overcome-it-172466.

2. Penberthy, "Regret Can Be."

3. *About Time*, directed by Richard Curtis (London: Working Title Films, 2013), Blu-ray Disc.

Chapter 3 Anxiety Monsters

1. *Oxford Learner's Dictionary*, s.v. "demystify," accessed January 9, 2023, https://www.oxfordlearnersdictionaries.com/us/definition/english/demystify.

2. "Using Your Most Critical Self-Defense Tool: Your Voice," Strategic Living, accessed November 11, 2022, https://www.strategicliving.org/using-your-voice/.

3. "Stage Fright? You're Not Alone! 5 Famous Singers Who Still Get Nervous," Songbird Studios, April 1, 2017, https://songbirdsf.com/5-famous-singers-who -still-get-stage-fright/.

4. Jeryl Brunner, "On the Anniversary of FDR's Birth, Read His 15 Greatest Quotes," *Parade*, January 30, 2015, https://parade.com/370879/jerylbrunner/on -the-anniversary-of-fdrs-birth-read-his-15-greatest-quotes/.

5. John Bevere, *The Awe of God: The Astounding Way a Healthy Fear of God Transforms Your Life* (Nashville: Thomas Nelson, 2023), 13.

Chapter 4 Breaking Comparisons

1. Tiffany McDougall, "Pools of Bethesda," Carleton University, May 14, 2014, https://carleton.ca/studyisrael/2014/tiffany-mcdougall-pools-bethesda/.

2. Martin Bailey, "How Did the Only Painting Sold by Van Gogh in His Lifetime End up in Russia?," *The Art Newspaper*, February 4, 2022, https://www .theartnewspaper.com/2022/02/04/how-did-the-only-painting-sold-by-van-gogh -in-his-lifetime-end-up-in-russia.

Chapter 5 The Shame Game

1. AsapSCIENCE, "Do You Hear 'Yanny' or 'Laurel'? (SOLVED with SCIENCE)," YouTube, May 16, 2018, https://www.youtube.com/watch?v=yDiXQ l7grPQ.

2. "What Is the Brain's Role in Hearing?," Discover Hearing, https://www .discoverhearing.ca/what-is-the-brains-role-in-hearing.

3. *Star Wars: Episode IV—New Hope*, directed by George Lucas (1977; Beverly Hills, CA: 20th Century Fox, 2011), Blu-ray Disc.

Chapter 6 The Broken Myth of "Enough"

1. Philip Kosloski, "How St. Barbara Was the Original 'Rapunzel,'" Aleteia, December 4, 2018, https://aleteia.org/2018/12/04/how-st-barbara-was-the-original -rapunzel/.

2. Larry D. Rosen, "Phantom Pocket Vibration Syndrome," *Psychology Today*, May 7, 2013, https://www.psychologytoday.com/us/blog/rewired-the-psychology -technology/201305/phantom-pocket-vibration-syndrome.

3. "Pledge to Unplug: The Health Benefits of Curbing Your Digital Independence," The Daily Dose, March 9, 2018, https://blog.cdphp.com/healthy-living /pledge-to-unplug-the-health-benefits-of-curbing-your-digital-dependence/.

4. "Brain Chemistry and the Secret Power of Texting," Regroup, November 29, 2016, https://www.regroup.com/blog/brain-chemistry-and-the-secret-power -of-texting/.

5. *Mean Girls*, directed by Mark Waters (Hollywood, CA: Paramount Home Entertainment, 2009), Blu-ray Disc.

6. "Q & A: Billy Graham's Warning against an Epidemic of 'Easy Believism,'" *Christianity Today*, October 15, 2013, https://www.christianitytoday.com/ct/2013 /october-web-only/billy-graham-interview-my-hope-easy-believism.html.

7. Jonathan Young, "A Day to Honor Saint Barbara," Center for Story and Symbol, November 30, 1997, https://folkstory.com/articles/stbabs.html.

Chapter 7 Liar, Liar

1. Sun Tzu, *The Art of War* (Minneapolis: Filiquarian, 2007), 7.
2. Tzu, *The Art of War*, 15.
3. Vanessa Van Edwards, "Mirroring Body Language: 4 Steps to Successfully Mirror Others," Science of People, accessed January 10, 2023, https://www.science ofpeople.com/mirroring/.

Chapter 8 Help My Unbelief

1. @tino.social, "When God Blesses You #word #inspiring #steveharvey #social central," TikTok, December 12, 2022, https://www.tiktok.com/@tino.social/video /7179317498523700485.

Chapter 9 Actually, We Can't Stay Friends

1. "William James," Heroic, accessed November 29, 2022, https://www.heroic .us/optimize/quotes/william-james/the-greatest-discovery-of-our-generation-is -that-human-beings.
2. "10 Facts about Michelangelo's Statue of David in Florence, Italy," Context, accessed November 29, 2022, https://www.contexttravel.com/blog/articles/ten -facts-about-the-statue-of-david.
3. Gina Edwards, "7 Types of Conflict in Literature: How to Use Them (with Examples)," Pro Writing Aid, August 7, 2020, https://prowritingaid.com/art/1366 /what-are-the-7-types-of-conflict-in-literature.aspx.
4. *Oxford Learner's Dictionary*, s.v. "change," accessed January 10, 2023, https://www.oxfordlearnersdictionaries.com/us/definition/english/change_1.
5. *Oxford Learner's Dictionary*, s.v. "change."
6. "The Power of Emotional Intelligence," ABC Training, accessed January 10, 2023, https://www.trainingabc.com/the-power-of-emotional-intelligence/#:~:text =People%20with%20emotional%20intelligence%20use%20criticism%20to%20 their%20benefit.,find%20ways%20to%20improve%20yourself.
7. "Everything You Need to Know about NASCAR Pit Stops," Pittalks, January 15, 2022, https://pittalks.com/nascar-pit-stop/.
8. Simon Sinek, *Start with Why: How Great Leaders Inspire Everyone to Take Action* (New York: Portfolio, 2011), 80.
9. Chris Melore, "Does Your Social Circle Measure Up? Survey Finds Average Adult Has 10 Good Friends," StudyFinds, July 29, 2022, https://studyfinds.org /average-adult-10-good-friends/.
10. "Are Friends Better than Family for Your Health?," VOA Learning English, accessed November 29, 2022, https://learningenglish.voanews.com/a/health -lifestyle-friends-or-family/3952739.html.
11. "What's the Difference between Sugar Free and No Sugar Added?," American Heart Association, accessed January 10, 2023, https://www.heart.org

/en/healthy-living/healthy-eating/eat-smart/sugar/difference-between-sugar-free
-and-no-added-sugar.

12. Isaac Eliaz, "7 Reasons You Probably Have an Unhealthy Gut (and 5 Ways to Improve Gut Health)," Dr. Axe, October 10, 2022, https://draxe.com/health /gut-health/.

13. Associated Press, "A Euro Is Worth Less than a Dollar for the First Time in 20 Years. What Does That Mean?," *Los Angeles Times*, August 23, 2022, https:// www.latimes.com/business/story/2022-08-23/euro-falls-below-parity-dollar.

14. "Positive Thinking: Stop Negative Self-Talk to Reduce Stress," Mayo Clinic, accessed November 30, 2022, https://www.mayoclinic.org/healthy-lifestyle /stress-management/in-depth/positive-thinking/art-20043950.

15. "Why the Giant Sequoia Needs Fire to Grow," PBS, accessed November 30, 2020, https://www.pbs.org/wnet/nature/giant-sequoia-needs-fire-grow/15094/.

Chapter 10 Your Prince Charming Is Waiting

1. Amanda O'Neill, "Dr. Estelle Lazer in Pompeii," Ancient History School, accessed December 1, 2022, https://www.ancienthistoryschool.com/blog/2019 /3/21/dr-estelle-lazer-in-pompeii.

Chapter 11 You Have a Testimony

1. Nargis Sultana, "Right to Education for Girls in Pakistan: Malala's Struggle Must Continue," Open Society Foundations, October 19, 2012, https://www.open societyfoundations.org/voices/und-49.

2. "Afghanistan: Taliban Deprive Women of Livelihoods, Identity," Human Rights Watch, January 18, 2022, https://www.hrw.org/news/2022/01/18/afghani stan-taliban-deprive-women-livelihoods-identity.

3. Sultana, "Right to Education for Girls."

4. Malala Yousafzai, "Malala Yousafzai: 16th Birthday Speech at the United Nations," speech, United Nations, July 12, 2013, New York, NY, https://malala .org/newsroom/malala-un-speech.

5. "Malala Yousafzai Fund—How Much Money Has the Malala Fund Raised?," Impulse Financial, June 25, 2022, https://impulsionfinance.com/malala-yousafzai -fund-how-much-money-has-the-malala-fund-raised/.

6. Hilary Weaver, "The World's Most Expensive Painting Sold at Auction Is Missing, and the Louvre Abu Dhabi Isn't Panicking," *Vanity Fair*, January 9, 2019, https://www.vanityfair.com/style/2019/01/the-mystery-of-salvator-mundi.

7. Weaver, "The World's Most Expensive Painting."

Chapter 12 Nobody's Damsel in Distress

1. *Cambridge Dictionary*, s.v. "a damsel in distress," accessed January 26, 2023, https://dictionary.cambridge.org/us/dictionary/english/damsel-in-distress.

2. Áine Cain, "28 Weird Jobs Famous People Had before Making It Big," *Insider*, November 17, 2016, https://www.businessinsider.com/weird-jobs-famous -people-had-before-making-it-big-2016-11#the-pope-was-a-bouncer-3.

3. "Stinger Removal," MedlinePlus, accessed November 10, 2022, https://med lineplus.gov/ency/imagepages/19629.htm.

4. C. S. Lewis, *The Problem of Pain* in The C. S. Lewis Signature Classics (San Francisco: HarperOne, 2017), 604.

5. "Myrtle," Plant Site, accessed December 7, 2022, https://ww2.odu.edu /~lmusselm/plant/bible/myrtle.php.

6. Erin Blakemore, "The Disastrous Backstory behind the Invention of LEGO Bricks," *History*, accessed December 6, 2022, https://www.history.com/news/the -disastrous-backstory-behind-the-invention-of-lego-bricks.

7. Dave Schefcik, "LEGO Named World's Most Powerful Brand by Global 500 Rankings," The Brothers Brick, February 1, 2017, https://www.brothers-brick .com/2017/02/01/lego-named-worlds-powerful-brand-global-500-rankings-news/.

8. "Toys 25 2022 Ranking," Brand Finance, accessed December 6, 2022, https:// brandirectory.com/rankings/toys.

9. Charles Dickens, *Great Expectations* (London: East India Publishing Company, 2020), 412.

Christian Bevere is passionate about seeing women discover their identity in Christ. A firm believer in God's redemption story, she shares powerful truth and practical applications through her books, podcast, online platform, and teachings. Wife to Arden Bevere and mother to Azariah Jax Bevere, she's seen firsthand how God's graciousness enables us to live in the abundance of His goodness. Bevere is on a mission to help others encounter God, silence shame, and avoid settling for less than His best. You can learn more about Christian Bevere at HusbandsBible.com or by following her on Instagram @MrsChristianBevere.

Meet the Author

CHRISTIAN BEVERE is an encourager, author, and podcaster who empowers women of all ages and backgrounds to pursue God's beautiful and perfect plan for their lives so they never have to settle for less. Find more curated content on her Instagram page and YouTube channel.

CONNECT WITH CHRISTIAN

 @MrsChristianBevere   @TheBeveres

YOUR JOURNEY TO A THRIVING RELATIONSHIP STARTS HERE.

Content designed to shape your singleness and strengthen your (future) relationship.